TWO PORTUGUESE-AMERICAN PLAYS

TWO PORTUGUESE-AMERICAN PLAYS

Edited by Patricia A. Thomas

AMARELO
Paulo A. Pereira

THROUGH A PORTAGEE GATE
Patricia A. Thomas
*(Adapted from the memoir of the same title
by Charles Reis Felix.)*

Center for Portuguese Studies and Culture
University of Massachusetts Dartmouth
North Dartmouth, Massachusetts
2008

PORTUGUESE IN THE AMERICAS SERIES 9
General Editor: Frank F. Sousa
Editor: Patricia A. Thomas
Copyeditor: Richard Larschan
Editorial Manager: Gina M. Reis
Graphic Designer: Spencer Ladd

Distributed by Amazon.com

Permission to perform/produce either play before an audience, whether paying or not, must be sought by writing to Culture Park Theatre, 69 Walden Street, New Bedford, MA 02740.

Two Portuguese-American plays: Amarelo / by Paulo A. Pereira ; Through a Portagee Gate / by Patricia A. Thomas (adapted from the memoir of the same title by Charles Reis Felix).
p. cm.—(Portuguese in the Americas series 9)
ISBN 1-933227-21-4 (pbk.: alk. paper)
1. American drama—Portuguese American authors. 2. Portuguese Americans—Drama. 3. Immigrants—United States—Drama.
I. Pereira, Paulo A. Amarelo II. Thomas, Patricia A. Through a Portagee Gate. III. Felix, Charles Reis. Through a Portagee Gate. IV. University of Massachusetts Dartmouth Center for Portuguese Studies and Culture.
PS634.2T96 2007
812.608—dc22
2007030412

Table of Contents

In 1971, when Conceição, the protagonist-narrator of Paulo A. Pereira's   *vii*
memory play, *Amarelo*, followed her husband Luís's dream and immi-
grated to the United States, Charlie Chaplin had long since produced a
string of movies, including "The Immigrant," his tale of sacrifice in
quest for the American Dream. José Felix, the immigrant in Charles
Reis Felix's multi-layered memoir, *Through a Portagee Gate*, had preced-
ed Conceição by nearly fifty years; but unlike Conceição, who accompan-
ied her new husband, José Felix journeyed on his own from Setúbal,
Portugal. A shoemaker like his father before him, and his father before
that, José Felix arrived with nothing but the shirt on his back and the
shoe-making skills passed on to him. In pursuit of work, and hoping to
prosper, José, and later Conceição and Luís, settled in New Bedford,
Massachusetts, a textile mill city of nearly 100,000 people, most of
whom, much like José, had left behind poverty and lack of opportunity
to pursue the elusive American Dream.

These two plays offer views of the immigrant experience as seen
through the lives of their Portuguese-speaking protagonists. In *Through
a Portagee Gate*, José Felix works day and night to amass his savings,
traveling to banks across town so that no one will "suspect" the size of
his bankroll. José's wife, Ilda, teases him—"he's like an old lady down
there in that shop gossiping"—but is duly devoted. She would love to
go back to Portugal where they could "live like kings," but José isn't con-
vinced. Young Charley dreams of being one of the "real Americans,"
whom he joins on the college track at New Bedford High School where
he is far enough away from his North End immigrant neighbors. He
eventually leaves New Bedford to attend the University of Michigan,
then Stanford, and beyond—settling in California. Charles would

never reside in New Bedford again. "Masquerading as an American," he is nevertheless consumed with writing about the world of his childhood. The play recounts the journey of Charley—Charles Reis Felix, narrator of the memoir—as he faces his roots in the form of a Portuguese-American custodian who cleans the classroom where he teaches in Escamil, California.

In *Amarelo*, a starry-eyed Conceição and her new husband, Luís Cordeiro, emigrate from their tiny village of Covoada on the island of São Miguel in the Azores to a tenement apartment (a "Portuguese basement") in New Bedford. They find work in fish and munitions plants, start a family, and never look back—that is, until Conceição's son, too, leaves home. The play begins as Conceição recounts the journey of her life and the choices she has made. She wants to feel something—"something to hold on to"—just to be sure. Conceição personifies the sentiment "saudade," the celebrated Portuguese word referring to nostalgia and longing, tinged with a profound sadness.

Though different in texture and style, these two Portuguese-American plays have similar themes, even if dissimilar outcomes. Both reflect upon parent-child relationships, and each examines the process of assimilation into working-class America. *Amarelo* is a poetic tale—a memory play—sparsely told, with minimal set and costumes, while *Through a Portagee Gate* is a rich, epic story spanning most of the twentieth century, with a colorful cast of characters who visit José Felix's cobbler shop. The Radio Ensemble at the WNBH studio in New Bedford punctuates the action and takes us through the century-long journey. Both plays depict the challenges of assimilation and the potentially triumphant outcome of forging a new life in America.

As for "The Immigrant," both Conceição Amarelo and José Felix identified with Charlie Chaplin. They, and their immigrant peers, felt a connection to him—perhaps a security in knowing that their struggle to achieve a dream with America at its center could be approached with humor and humanity.

Patricia A. Thomas

AMARELO

Paulo A. Pereira

For Alexandrina, Guida and Paula Cristina.

"We'll see how brave you are.
We'll see how fast you'll be running."
—Tori Amos

Amarelo was first produced as a workshop by the MIT Theater Arts Department. It was performed in Kresge Auditorium, Rehearsal Room B, on October 20 and 21, 1995. Prof. Brenda Cotto-Escalera directed the cast of Charles Armesto, Jaqueline Brener, Natalia Fuentes, Rick McKern and the voices of Tara Perry and the author.

Amarelo was produced in New York City by Synergy at the Theatre-Studio, Inc., where it opened on April 4, 1998 with the following cast:

Conceição	Toni D'Antonio
Manuel	Sean McEwen
Natália	Illiam Carrillo
Alexandre	Joe Carapella
Luís	William Hernandez
Man	Socrates Diamant

It was directed by Charles Armesto, with Beth Turomsha as design consultant. John Salisbury was stage manager. Props and costumes were by Michelle Starz-Gaiano. Original music (for Grain of Salt) was written and performed by Julianne Sutton & Christopher DeMaria.

Amarelo was presented by Culture*Park Theatre and Performing Arts Collaborative of New Bedford, Massachusetts, sponsored by the University of Massachusetts Dartmouth Center for Portuguese Studies and Culture, on April 12 & 13, 2003, with the following cast:

Conceição	Susan Perfetto
Manuel	Matthew Lecuyer
Natália	Shannon Gracia
Alexandre	Ben Jolivet
Luís	Michael Ventura
Man	Fred Cabral

It was directed by Patricia A. Thomas. Rebecca Schade was production designer. Costume design was by Niko Tarini. Ivone Rego and Joseph Twomey were stage managers.

Maria da Conceição Ferreira Amarelo   *9*
a woman from the Azores

Manuel Alexandre Amarelo Cordeiro
Maria da Conceição's son

Natália Maria Ferreira Amarelo
Maria da Conceição's sister

Alexandre Costa
Maria da Conceição's friend

Luís Resendes Cordeiro
Maria da Conceição's husband

Man

ACT ONE

The set and costumes should be as minimalist as possible, except where noted. The temporal leaps and setting changes should come across primarily through the players and through shifts in the lighting, as indicated in the stage directions. The story is to be told fluidly.

The Man character may be used freely and creatively as a story-telling device and as a mechanism to keep the narrative moving forward. Besides taking on the roles of several minor characters, the Man can be used to actualize set pieces and might even function as a stagehand.

12   *The play begins with* CONCEIÇÃO *sitting center stage in a pool of light. She takes a moment.* MANUEL *enters and stands near the periphery of the illuminated area.*

New Bedford, Massachusetts, 1991.

CONCEIÇÃO
(*Not harshly.*) Sit down, Manuel.

MANUEL
You wanted to see me?

CONCEIÇÃO
Yes. Sit down.

MANUEL
Ma, please. I don't wanna part on a sour note. Let's just… 13

CONCEIÇÃO
Manuel Alexandre Amarelo Cordeiro…

MANUEL
Here we go. What did I tell ya?

CONCEIÇÃO
Please. Sit down. (**MANUEL** *does not move. Pause.*) I want things to change, I want this to change, between us.

MANUEL
Ma, it's my last night in New Bedford. Things don't change like that. (*Pause.* **CONCEIÇÃO** *begins to laugh.*) What? (**CONCEIÇÃO** *continues laughing.*) What?

CONCEIÇÃO
(*Breathes deeply to regain composure.*) Sit down.

MANUEL
(*Pause. Quietly.*) I've still got a ton of packing to finish up. I vote we save the sad good-byes for tomorrow. (*Turns to leave.*)

CONCEIÇÃO
I have a long history of atrociously mangled good-byes. Not this time. Manuel Alexandre. Manuel. Manny! (**MANUEL** *stops.*) One last story.

One last chance. (*Pause.*) Sit. (*Pause.* MANUEL *sits. Pause.*) It's strange which memories will stay with you. It's as if life were made up of only a handful of significant moments—the times when your life has veered off in new directions. (*Beat.*) But, sometimes the paths you take aren't as important as the reasons why you took them.

MANUEL
Ma, I really don't understand what…

CONCEIÇÃO
Shhhhh. No, don't talk. Listen.

The lights become tightly focused on CONCEIÇÃO. MANUEL *joins the audience, which* CONCEIÇÃO *now addresses.*

CONCEIÇÃO
The only place to start is with Natália. My childhood with Natália. Yes, she was my older sister, my only sister, but even more so, she was my baptismal godmother. My *madrinha*. She was like a mother to me when I was a young girl. Ma-mãe was there too, and she was a caring parent, please don't misunderstand me, but, well, I suppose she had her hands full with the boys. I had five older brothers living in the house for most of my childhood. And, of course, being boys, they caused much more trouble than me. So she had to keep an eye on them, while I went about my business, went to school, completed my chores—most of the time, back then, in Natália's company. (NATÁLIA *enters.*) .

NATÁLIA
(*Not harshly.*) Conceição, don't sing while you set the table—you may become distracted. (*Beat.*) Conceição, if you're going to sing while you set the table, don't dance—you'll drop the bowls. (*Beat.*) Conceição— off the table—now! (*Pause.*) Conceição, you must listen. Shhhhh. No, don't talk. Listen.

CONCEIÇÃO
She'd lift me into her arms and search my eyes.

14

NATÁLIA
What are you thinking? (**CONCEIÇÃO** *giggles. Pause*) Conceição.
Sãozinha. I will be leaving soon. I am engaged. (*Beat.*) To be married.

CONCEIÇÃO
To a man? (*Pause.*) I couldn't understand how she could have had time
for anything else.

Lighting shift. São Miguel, Açores, 1959.

NATÁLIA   15
(*Pause.*) Yes, yes, Mãe, it was all in the letter. (*Beat.*) Oh yes, Mário, I
was quite surprised. (*Beat.*) I'm not sure, Pai, I assume that José will find
a home for us there in America. There is so much space there. (*Beat.*)
Oh, I don't know about that, Filipe, I don't think it will be a mansion—
but José is working very hard. (*Beat.*) No, Octávio, I do not believe I
will be living anywhere near Charlie Chaplin.

CONCEIÇÃO
Charlie Chaplin lives in Switzerland now. (*Beat.*) Does so! (*Beat.*)
Does so!

NATÁLIA
Maria da Conceição!

CONCEIÇÃO
He does! I read it in one of Pai's old newspapers! I don't care what you
say! You'll never see him! Never! (*Runs off.*)

NATÁLIA
No, Mãe, everything is fine. It is close to her bedtime, anyway. (*Beat.*)
No, do not worry yourself, Mãe; I will speak with her. (*Pause.*)

The MAN *enters.* NATÁLIA *takes a moment alone with* HIM.

NATÁLIA
Someone to fill every moment with something to think about. I could
shut my eyes and scream and keep screaming for the rest of my life! I
have waited my whole life for this to happen. Everything is working out
perfectly. Right now, I cannot remember any other dream I have had—
ever! (*The* MAN *begins to approach* NATÁLIA, *but* SHE *turns away.*)
Sāozinha.

CONCEIÇÃO
The next three months leading up to Madrinha's departure, I refused to
talk about America, or anything pertaining to America. Especially José.
(*Beat.*) I even filled in the United States with black ink on Pai's desktop
globe so that it would blend in with the oceans. I thought I was going
to get the spanking of my life. But Pai just laughed when he saw it. He
asked me if I was working for the Russians.

Lighting shift. CONCEIÇÃO *is in bed.* NATÁLIA *sits beside* HER. *This
is now the night before* NATÁLIA *is to leave. The* MAN *poses as explorer*
VELHO. HE *acts out the story of* VELHO, *but mostly* HE *stands there
looking regal.*

NATÁLIA
… So then, Prince Henry sent his best man, Friar Gonçalo Velho, to
investigate this new, uncharted island. The Friar carefully set a course to
the coordinates of the little land mass, which had been reported to the
Prince by a merchant ship, as the law demanded. He hoped to claim
new soil for His Liege and His God, and imagined a beautiful land of
dense foliage and thick dark sand, like the other colonies in Africa and
America. However, when they arrived there after eight long weeks at
sea, the Friar and his men were quite disappointed by what greeted
them. Santa Maria, as the sailors had come to refer to it (expecting to
arrive as they did during Our Lady's Month of May), actually seemed to
be nothing more than ugly burnt-looking rock jutting out from under
the ocean. The vegetation was scarce and mostly brown, and the cliffs
surrounding much of the island were steep and quite ominous in
appearance. The sailors became sullen and requested that the ship be
turned around immediately, but the Friar would not hear of it. He con-

16

vinced the men to make the best of the situation, reminding them to keep their faith in the Lord. (**VELHO** *produces a whip.*) Reinvigorated by the Friar's eloquence, the seamen sailed the ship around the island and soon found a good place to set anchor, not far from a short stretch of sand where they could easily go ashore. Which is exactly what these well-trained holy men did, officially claiming Santa Maria as Portuguese land. The Friar was proud of his men for not giving in to their pride and disappointment, and granted them a few days of rest before returning back to report their findings to Prince Henry. Tired from their long journey, they all agreed that they could use the time to better explore the rocky little isle (which would likely please the Prince) and to prepare themselves for the return voyage. Noticing that the sun and its reflection were about to meet, the men set up camp on the beach and were all asleep before the sky had turned completely black. However, their rest was to be short-lived.

CONCEIÇÃO
Oooooh, I can't wait, I can't wait! Let me see if I can tell the rest of the story myself. I've got it all in my head. I have a great memory.

NATÁLIA *relinquishes the role of narrator.* VELHO *is now under* CONCEIÇÃO's *control, to her delight.* HE *has some trouble keeping up.*

CONCEIÇÃO
Friar Gonçalo woke up, and he saw an island—São Miguel—but he didn't know it was called São Miguel yet, and he didn't wake up his men because he was...'dumfounded by the Golden Light of Heaven.' Oh, the Golden Light of Heaven...the Golden Light of Heaven is what allowed him to see São Miguel, but it wasn't called São Miguel yet. So he went back to the ship...no, no, he woke up all his men, first, and then they all returned to the ship. Together. (*Pause.*)

NATÁLIA
What is wrong?

CONCEIÇÃO
I know so far I've missed 'lit up as brilliantly as a thousand stars' and

'little peaceful green island waiting to be found, reclining on the horizon like a sleeping girl.'

NATÁLIA
That is fine. Go on.

CONCEIÇÃO
Oh, they collected their supplies and then returned to the ship! That's it. And they sailed off to the little island. 'The men cheered for this lush oasis of forest in the desert of the blue-black sea.' It was beautiful, nothing like Santa Maria. It was springtime and all the flowers were blooming and the trees were singing and there were rabbits! Big rabbits!

NATÁLIA *is unimpressed and continues the story from there, much to* **VELHO'S** *relief.*

NATÁLIA
When Friar Gonçalo stepped onto the shore, the men became solemn and knelt before their brave leader, for in his hands he held the Portuguese flag and a golden crucifix mounted on a long staff.

VELHO
In the name of Jesus Christ, Our Sovereign King, and of His Servant Prince Infante Dom Henrique, I claim this land for the Holy Portuguese Empire!

NATÁLIA
And just as the cross and the flag were thrust into the sand, the sky erupted a second time, and bathed in the ethereal glow was an image of São Miguel, the Archangel and Champion Warrior of Heaven!

CONCEIÇÃO
Rrrrrraghhhrrrr!

VELHO *exits, running.*

18

NATÁLIA
Excuse me?

CONCEIÇÃO
Sorry.

NATÁLIA
Well, anyway, they all realize that it is the eighth day of May, which is of course…

CONCEIÇÃO
The Feast Day of the Apparition of São Miguel!

NATÁLIA
And…

CONCEIÇÃO
…and they name the whole island after him! Close?

NATÁLIA
Close enough.

CONCEIÇÃO
Yay! I must have made you tell me that story a million times since I was a little, little girl.

NATÁLIA
At least.

CONCEIÇÃO
I like that story so much.

NATÁLIA
Yes, I know you do. That fact has disturbed both your mother and me for quite some time. Button up that nightdress like a good girl.

CONCEIÇÃO
I only like it when you tell it. You're the only one who can get every-thing right every time. And I like the way you do São Miguel coming down from heaven to scare the sailors…

NATÁLIA
Maria da Conceição! That is not why he comes down from heaven, and you know it!

CONCEIÇÃO
That's how I see it.

NATÁLIA
Yes, and when I try to teach you Portuguese history, you root for the Moors!

CONCEIÇÃO
It doesn't make a difference! Dom Afonso Henriques wins every time, anyway!

NATÁLIA
No thanks to this little warrior! Now, after I am gone, you will not be difficult with Mãe as you have been with me. You will listen to her respectfully.

CONCEIÇÃO
Madrinha, must you leave tomorrow?

NATÁLIA
Yes, I must. You know that. Now listen. Mãe is very busy, and will not be able to tolerate foolishness as I do. Please tell me you will grow up a little. You will have to. With one less woman around, you will have to take on more chores around the house, on top of your schoolwork. You must therefore be more responsible. Do not waste time arguing with your brothers. You are no longer a baby, Conceição. You're twelve years old! You're a young woman! You are old enough to realize the sacrifices Pai is making to keep you in school. You have to be—look at me—you

have to be a serious girl. Don't tell Mãe you want to go explore Africa with Prince Henry.

CONCEIÇÃO
Why must you go?

NATÁLIA
You haven't been listening at all!

CONCEIÇÃO
Yes, I have. Don't tell Ma-mãe that I want to explore Prince Henry. *21*

NATÁLIA
That's not funny! Don't say things like that!

CONCEIÇÃO
Madrinha, I'm sorry. I was listening.

NATÁLIA
Oh, Sãozinha, you silly girl. I have done a terrible job of raising you.

CONCEIÇÃO
No, don't be sad. Please. That's not true. You have taken very good care of me. You are the only one who takes good care of me. I have learned everything you've read to me, everything you've taught me! But that is why you must stay here with me! I won't learn from anyone else.

NATÁLIA
Conceição, please, if you love me, do not say that. Listen to Mãe carefully. And Pai. (*Pause.*) You will make them happy. Am I right?

CONCEIÇÃO
Yes, Madrinha. I promise to be good.

NATÁLIA
You promise to make Mãe and Pai happy?

Conceição
(*Pause.*) I promise to make Mãe and Pai happy.

Natália
Good girl. (*Hug.*)

Conceição
I want to be just like you when I grow up! You have everything! You're so beautiful! Ma-mãe always says that you will make a wonderful wife and mother. You're so grown up! You have everything you want!

Natália
(*Quietly.*) My heart is filled with peace and happiness. That is why the Lord has blessed me. But, He calls me away. Away from my family in São Miguel. To be married, and to live a new life in America with my husband. I will have my own family now. But these blessings would not have been bestowed upon me if I had not found peace. I want you to feel that same peace, Sãozinha.

Conceição
You know what? I think the Lord is calling me to go with you.

Natália
No, He is not! Get back into bed! (**They** *share a laugh. Pause.*) You. You you you you you. (*Almost whispered.*) Do not aspire to be me, *querida.* I want you to be much more. (*She kisses* **Conceição**.)

Conceição
Madrinha, I don't…

Natália
Shhhhh. Go to sleep now. I will see you tomorrow morning before I leave. I will miss you, Sãozinha. I will miss you. (*Exits.*)

Conceição
(*Rising from bed, addressing the audience again.*) I suddenly have no idea what I'm doing anymore.

MAN *enters with* ALEXANDRE *and positions* HIM *on stage.*
CONCEIÇÃO *does not see them.*

ALEXANDRE
(*To* MAN.) I will not "mingle" with these people.

CONCEIÇÃO
I have to find something to hold on to.

ALEXANDRE
Well, maybe I'm not interested.   23

CONCEIÇÃO
Something that won't go away.

ALEXANDRE
No! That's not what I meant! Don't say that!

MAN *exits.*

CONCEIÇÃO
Something that will keep me alive.

ALEXANDRE
(*Quietly, to himself.*) I don't care who you are. Don't ever say that.

Lighting shift. CONCEIÇÃO *bumps into* ALEXANDRE. *It is now four years later, 1963.*

CONCEIÇÃO
Oh my. I beg your pardon.

ALEXANDRE
(*Recognizes* CONCEIÇÃO. *Under his breath.*) I'm sure.

CONCEIÇÃO
I'll be right there to help you to serve the *sopas,* Ma-mãe! (*Pause.*)

Excuse me? (*Beat.*) Excuse me?

ALEXANDRE
You're excused already. Go help your mother.

CONCEIÇÃO
In a minute, Ma-mãe! (*Pause.*) No, I mean, what did you say?

ALEXANDRE
Nothing.

CONCEIÇÃO
No, you did so.

ALEXANDRE
So?

CONCEIÇÃO
You're one of the Costas. Alexandre, right? (*Beat.*) Why, hello, it's a pleasure to make your acquaintance, I am…

ALEXANDRE
I know who you are. Everyone knows who you are.

CONCEIÇÃO
You're silly.

ALEXANDRE
Senhor Amarelo's youngest. The first girl from Covoada to go to school in Ponta Delgada. The prettiest girl in the village. Blah blah blah. Blah blah blah.

CONCEIÇÃO
You know, it's hard to make friends going to school in the city as I do. Did you know I had to walk the whole way there and back for two years? Two whole years! Pai said it built my character. But Ma-mãe didn't like it. She said walking that far everyday would make my ankles

too thick. And the rest of me too skinny. And then who would want me? Ma-mãe's always thinking ahead like that. (*Pause.*) Yes, I hear you, Ma-mãe! I'm over here! (*Pause.*) Would you like to try 'discussing things,' like the adults? What things would you like to discuss? I read Pai's newspapers, so I'm caught up on current events. Have you noticed that most of the men are discussing the revolutionary movements in the African territories and most of the women are standing in the kitchen complaining about the men? Isn't that something? I think I'd rather talk about the pending wars than about the men, but then if you think about it, the war will only be fought by men, so either way I guess I'd be talking about men, right? I never thought about it that way before. (*Pause.*) Oh! You go ahead, Ma-mãe! Sorry! (*Pause.*)

ALEXANDRE *is staring at* CONCEIÇÃO. SHE *stares right back.*

ALEXANDRE
What?

CONCEIÇÃO
You're very interesting. The rest of your family is enjoying their *Domingo do Espírito Santo,* and you're standing here sulking.

ALEXANDRE
That's right, it's ours! Our *Domingo!* It was my little sister who was crowned this morning! (*Beat.*) And we're having dinner at your house!

CONCEIÇÃO
But your mother…

ALEXANDRE
I know what she did. She's ashamed of what we have. Of our home.

CONCEIÇÃO
They always use our house like a church hall. We have the space.

ALEXANDRE
I've never felt so humiliated. Why should I be ashamed of who I am?

(*Pause.* **She** *is staring again.*) What!?

Music for the sapateia begins playing from off-stage.

CONCEIÇÃO
Oh no. You. You have to help me.

ALEXANDRE
What? What is it?

CONCEIÇÃO
The *sapateia*. Ma-mãe warned me that I'd better not disappear this year.
Ever since my sister moved away, she expects me to represent the family
in the dance.

ALEXANDRE
I'm not stopping you.

CONCEIÇÃO
They always pair me up with that fat Resendes boy.

ALEXANDRE
And?

CONCEIÇÃO
And…and he looks at me too much. (*She tries to drag* **ALEXANDRE**
toward the music.)

ALEXANDRE
Wait a minute. I don't like to dance.

CONCEIÇÃO
Oh, that's right. You like to stand around by yourself and mutter. (**SHE**
tries again.)

ALEXANDRE
No, I'm serious. I can't dance.

Conceição
Everyone can dance the *sapateia*. Pai says it's in the blood of every *micaelense*.

Alexandre
Didn't you hear me? I don't even want to be here!

Conceição
If I was standing around like a deaf rooster, I wouldn't want to be here either. Now do you want everyone to see you with 'the prettiest girl in the village,' or don't you?

27

Alexandre
(*Long pause.*) Just so you know, I don't like you.

Conceição
Good. I don't like you either. (*To audience.*) I remember that afternoon so clearly. I was all dressed up in my Sunday best, my favorite red flowing skirt. And new clogs that Pai agreed to buy for me just for the occasion, even though Ma-mãe had thought it was extravagant. *"Sapateia, meu bem, sapateia, ai, outra vez a sapateia…"*

Through the course of this story, **Conceição** *and* **Alexandre** *strike poses that suggest still photographs taken during the dance.*

Conceição
For some reason I started stomping harder and harder and everyone else stomped harder and harder and I smiled wider and wider until Alexandre couldn't help but laugh a little, and that made me laugh, but we kept stomping and stomping and we both couldn't stop laughing, and pretty soon all the dancers were laughing and stomping and everyone watching started laughing, and the musicians just played louder and we stomped even harder and the whole village seemed to be there howling together, when the music just… stopped. It was the end of the song of course. We all knew that. But something kept us all there just looking at each other. Looking at our partners. And we've been friends ever since.

CONCEIÇÃO *and* ALEXANDRE *run off.* HE *exits, but* SHE *is stopped short. Lighting shift. Six years later, 1969.*

VOICE OF CONCEIÇÃO'S FATHER
Conceição, o que estás a fazer!?

CONCEIÇÃO
(*Startled. Words come out as a reflex.*) Nothing, Pai. Nothing. I was just thinking.

VOICE OF CONCEIÇÃO'S FATHER
Well, stop doing nothing, and go entertain our guest on the veranda.

CONCEIÇÃO
Sim, senhor. (*To the audience.*) Where do all the years go? (SHE *refocuses herself.*) Of course. We just had dinner with Luís, the only son of Senhor Cordeiro. (MAN *positions* LUÍS *on stage and then exits.*) Senhor Cordeiro and Pai are *compadres;* Pai is godfather to Luís. He has just returned, earlier than expected, from his schooling on the mainland. Pai says he will be staying with us while his parents are…

VOICE OF CONCEIÇÃO'S FATHER
Eh, rapariga! Agora!

CONCEIÇÃO
Sim, Pai.

CONCEIÇÃO *approaches* LUÍS.

LUÍS
Olá.

CONCEIÇÃO
Hello.

LUÍS
Joining me?

CONCEIÇÃO
Yes. My father told me to accompany you.

LUÍS
Ah. I see. I would enjoy that.

CONCEIÇÃO
I'm sure my mother is busily preparing your room. And I believe my father said he had some reading to finish up.

LUÍS   29
Your father is an avid reader, an intelligent man, is he not?

CONCEIÇÃO
Yes! Yes, he is! Just because he is a farmer does not mean he is not smart!

LUÍS
No, of course…

CONCEIÇÃO
He taught himself to read, you know! He never went to school, and yet he has read more books than me, by far! That is why I want to go to university!

LUÍS
So that you will catch up to him?

CONCEIÇÃO
Because he is an inspiration to me. As he should be to the whole island.

LUÍS
What fierce loyalty. From what I understand, Padrinho has good reason to be proud of you, also.

CONCEIÇÃO
Sir?

Luís
Please, my name is Luís. I am only two or three years older than you, am I not?

Conceição
Yes, sir, I suppose.

Luís
Since I had the good fortune of meeting up with your father on the mainland before my trip back to the Açores, we traveled together, and he was kind enough to tell me many things about you.

Conceição
Is that so?

Luís
I understand you are the youngest teacher at the school in this village, yes?

Conceição
That's because the only other girl in Covoada to get past the fourth grade is already...

Luís
A wife and expectant mother?

Conceição
Yes.

Luís
So... why are...

Conceição
But you, you have studied at the Trás-os-Montes Seminary! That is a real education! Your head must be swimming with ideas!

Luís
You could say that.

Conceição
So you were intending on joining the priesthood?

Luís
Aaah... heh. Yes, Menina Conceição. Yes, I was. I was young then. And I did appreciate and take full advantage of the educational and spiritual guidance offered there. But both my advisor and I would come to realize that my calling... was elsewhere.

Conceição
Really? Where?

Luís
Elsewhere. That is what I am now searching for. (*Pause.*) God is calling me to start a family.

Conceição
Is He?

Luís
Yes. Yes, He is.

Conceição
Right now?

Luís
All the time.

Conceição
Oh. Tell me more about the seminary. No, no, tell me about the mainland!

Luís
Heh. Hmmm. The sky. The night sky. I spent much time on the mountain-

side grounds. The night sky is not like this on the mainland. There, it is just a faraway plane of stars. Here on São Miguel the sky appears to surround the whole island tightly, like a big black rubber ball poked with little holes.

CONCEIÇÃO
Perhaps that is why I don't seem to be able to get off São Miguel. I keep bouncing off the rubber ball.

LUÍS
Yes! Yes! Yes.

CONCEIÇÃO
Hmmm.

LUÍS
You want to leave?

CONCEIÇÃO
Well, not right now. (*Pause.*) You see, what I would…

LUÍS
Someday, though?

CONCEIÇÃO
(*Pause.*) I have certain dreams.

LUÍS
Me too! Me too! The future is an exciting place. A bit frightening.

CONCEIÇÃO
A little.

LUÍS
I need a brave woman to go with me there.

CONCEIÇÃO
Really? Maybe that's what I need, too.

Luís
You are an amusing girl. You make me smile.

Conceição
I must go to bed—I mean, go sleep, now.

Luís
Menina Conceição, please, wait! Have I offended you?

Conceição
No, sir, no.

33

Luís
Luís.

Conceição
I only feel that I should retire. Ma-mãe wouldn't like me out here so late.

Luís
Sãozinha, I would like us to be friends.

Conceição
Yes. That would be nice.

Luís
No, no, I mean that seriously. You are so... alive, my dear. I want to be near that kind of life. I have been away from it far too long. Your voice is sweeter than the porto we had at dinner. Your eyes glitter like an open treasure chest full of riches. You are so... alive! (*Pause.*) I apologize. I do not wish to sound foolish.

Conceição
Oh. Oh, no, no.

Luís
(*Pause.*) I just want to begin over... I know I can begin over now.

(*Pause.*) When my parents discover that I have left the seminary, my father will have me return to his fields. I am his only son. But I will not. I will never again plow or milk. And neither will my sons. (*Pause.*) I do sound foolish.

CONCEIÇÃO
We will be friends... Luís.

LUÍS
You go off to bed now. Don't let my senseless blather keep you up for one more minute. (*Beat.*) Will I give my friend a good-night kiss?

CONCEIÇÃO
(*Laughing.*) I do believe you will.

THEY *kiss.*

LUÍS
Boa noite. (*Exits.*)

CONCEIÇÃO
(*To the audience.*) Do people consider me "so alive"? I didn't know that. Well, maybe I did, a little. Pai usually just calls it "incorrigible." He likes to use big words. And he sometimes translates them into a couple different languages for you right there on the spot, just for effect.

ALEXANDRE *enters.*

CONCEIÇÃO
The times that I feel most alive, though, are in the mornings. On my way to the schoolhouse, I cut through the Costa family's fields. And I sneak behind the henhouse. And... Alexandre and I 'discuss things.'

ALEXANDRE
(*To the audience.*) I don't have many friends. The boys I grew up with all have families now. I never really had much in common with them, anyway. And I'm plenty busy working for my father. I don't have the time

for socializing. (*Pause.*) But, São, you look at me with those big brown eager eyes, as if you're just waiting for me to bare all the dark recesses of my soul.

CONCEIÇÃO
Oh, he gets in these philosophical moods sometimes. But he's the best. Listen to this. (*Beat.*) Alexandre?

ALEXANDRE
What is it, São?

35

CONCEIÇÃO
Shouldn't I be married? I mean, at my age, my sister had been married for two years, and already had her first son!

ALEXANDRE
São, we've been through this.

CONCEIÇÃO
I know. Let's go through it one more time.

ALEXANDRE
You're only twenty-two years old. All these rules about marriage—they're all artificial. Our parents grew up in a world where you had to get married young! There was no way around it. Marriages were arranged half the time, anyway. Plus, back then, families had so many children that if each child didn't leave after their obligatory sixteen years of working in the fields... well, it would just foul up the whole system.

CONCEIÇÃO
Alexandre is so smart. He's a lot like Pai. Aaaah... no, not like Pai.

ALEXANDRE
I should have never let her get too close.

Lighting shift. It is now the morning after the scene with **Luís,** *and* **CONCEIÇÃO** *walks over to meet with* **ALEXANDRE. HE** *is sitting on the* *ground.* **CONCEIÇÃO** *lays down a blanket and joins* **HIM.**

CONCEIÇÃO
Bom dia! Tell me, do my eyes glitter?

ALEXANDRE
What?

CONCEIÇÃO
Is my voice as sweet as wine?

ALEXANDRE
More like vinegar.

CONCEIÇÃO
Hey! You're so mean.

ALEXANDRE
Uh-huh.

CONCEIÇÃO
Oh, is it Grumpy Day? I didn't realize. I'll just go in early and prepare the lessons.

ALEXANDRE
No! No, please. Come back. I need to speak with you.

CONCEIÇÃO
So, my voice is like wine, then?

ALEXANDRE
Don't push it.

CONCEIÇÃO
What a night.

ALEXANDRE
You didn't have that Prince Henry dream again, did you?

CONCEIÇÃO
No. (*Pause.*) Oh, Alexandre. All I want…all I want…

ALEXANDRE
I know, I know. All you want is to be…

BOTH
…a Physics teacher!   *37*

CONCEIÇÃO
Oh! To go study in Coimbra! To learn about Everything. How
Everything Works. It's all Energy. I've started reading some of Pai's
books. Matter. Mass. Inertia. But everything comes back to Energy. I
could understand Everything. (*Pause.* **SHE** *sighs and puts her head in*
ALEXANDRE'S *lap.*) I'm Energy! You're Energy! Can you believe that?
And… I'll never figure it all out unless I go! (*Pause.*) But I don't think
it's going to happen anymore. Alexandre, I think I'm running out of
time.

ALEXANDRE
(*Getting up.*) 'Running out of time.' Oh, I knew it.

CONCEIÇÃO
Knew? Knew what?

ALEXANDRE
I knew what you were getting at today. Don't play games. Your questions. 'Do my eyes glitter?' Dreams. Yeah, I'll bet.

CONCEIÇÃO
I don't know what you're…

ALEXANDRE
Just what was the Cordeiro boy doing at your house?

CONCEIÇÃO
You mean Luís? Luís is not a boy!

ALEXANDRE
Oh, really? 'Luís is not a boy'?

CONCEIÇÃO
Alexandre, what is wrong with you?

ALEXANDRE
Nothing. Nothing is wrong with me. Why does everyone think something is wrong with me? I just want you to tell me what Luís was doing at your house last night.

CONCEIÇÃO
I told you yesterday that my father invited him to stay with us for a few days.

ALEXANDRE
Did he have anything to say to you?

CONCEIÇÃO
Yes, we spoke a bit.

ALEXANDRE
And?

CONCEIÇÃO
And he is a fine gentleman! I think we became friends.

ALEXANDRE
What, I'm not a 'gentleman'?

CONCEIÇÃO
Alexandre! What is this all about? Why are you using that tone of voice with me? You're scaring me.

ALEXANDRE
'Friends'? Friends! Ha! He wants you to marry him!

CONCEIÇÃO
Ridiculous.

ALEXANDRE
You think so? My father… my father… had some news for me this morning.

MAN enters as **ALEXANDRE'S FATHER**.

ALEXANDRE'S FATHER
So, Amarelo's daughter is finally going to get hers. The old man was over here. He's spreading the word all over the village. The Cordeiro boy, fresh back from the mainland, wants her. And let me tell you, he's got her. They probably want to keep all that land away from the rest of us, anyways. Haven't you been working on that one, boy? Why didn't you sink your claws in time? I could have used the dowry! What's wrong with you, eh? Get yourself a woman. (*Exits.*)

CONCEIÇÃO
Oh, no. I don't believe it. Oh, Pai.

ALEXANDRE
Yeah, right. I had better go attend to the chickens. The sow seems to be doing fine.

CONCEIÇÃO
Alexandre, don't you dare insult me! I have agreed to nothing!

ALEXANDRE
Maybe you should go tell that to Luís. (*Turns to leave.*)

CONCEIÇÃO
I don't understand you today. You make me feel ashamed. And small. You've always told me that I should never have to feel this way. That no

one should feel this way.

ALEXANDRE
(*Pause.*) I am getting older, Conceição. I am at an age where I should be married. Not just you—me too. Don't you know the names they call me in town? 'In town.' In my own home. (*Pause.*) I thought I would be able to quiet their voices. I thought you would help me. As you have helped me. I know you don't love me. And I don't love you. No, don't talk. I have to finish this, now. We could have arranged something. I would have let you go study in Coimbra. I would have helped you. You know that! And you. You would not have pressured me. You would have let me sort through everything I feel. All the dirty things inside of me. But now I know I was wrong. Your father must have told you. He believes what they say about me. And you believe him? How can you? I hate you!

CONCEIÇÃO
Stop. Stop! I don't understand what you're talking about. I don't want to understand. I don't recognize you today at all. I'm leaving.

ALEXANDRE
I won't be here tomorrow. I don't know where I'll be. (*Walks away.*)

CONCEIÇÃO
I don't care! I don't care!

BOTH *now address the audience.*

ALEXANDRE
I just don't care anymore. I can't.

CONCEIÇÃO
I can't! Oh my Lord—Luís! I can't marry someone I just met! Or can I? How can I?

ALEXANDRE
How can I…keep doing this? What's left for me here? I have nothing.

CONCEIÇÃO
I have nothing to hold on to. I'm not making much as a teacher.

ALEXANDRE
Nothing.

CONCEIÇÃO
Who knows when I could finally get to Coimbra? If ever.

ALEXANDRE
Nothing. (**HE** *pulls out a knife.*)   *41*

CONCEIÇÃO
All I can think about is what Alexandre said. And how angry he looked. And how dirty he looked. And Luís, last night. His eyes always seemed focused far away. As if he were scanning the horizon for a lost ship. The way I always pictured Prince Henry.

ALEXANDRE
I have nothing to hold on to.

ALEXANDRE *is interrupted by* **MAN**, *who enters wearing a Portuguese flag.* **MAN** *hands* **ALEXANDRE** *a telegram.* **ALEXANDRE** *reads part of it and crumples it in his hand.* **MAN** *extracts the telegram from* **ALEXANDRE**'S *fist and reads it aloud.*

MAN
Alexandre Costa. Covoada, São Miguel, Açores. This is a notice of conscription. You are summoned to fulfill your patriotic duty by joining your brothers-in-arms in the Portuguese National Army. You will report for training immediately at the National Army Base in Arrifes in preparation for your twenty-four months of mandatory active duty in the territory of Moçambique, on the African continent.

CONCEIÇÃO
A force is a physical quantity that can affect the motion of an object. If there is no net force acting on a body, it will continue in its state of rest

or will continue moving along a straight line with uniform speed.

ALEXANDRE *exits.* MAN *holds up the Portuguese flag for* CONCEIÇÃO.

CONCEIÇÃO
(*As if to her students.*) Settle down, children. As you all know, this is the Portuguese flag. The smaller green field signifies the hope of the people, and the larger red field represents the brave… the brave blood shed in expanding the empire and spreading the teachings of God's Church. The five pouches that form the cross in the center of the shield each contain five coins. Counting the middle pouch twice, that gives us the thirty coins for which Judas betrayed Our Lord Jesus Christ—a reminder of the evil of Satan, and the…

MAN
(*Impatiently.*)… and the temptation…

CONCEIÇÃO
… and the temptation… that lurks in each of us. The pouches can also be taken to symbolize the *cinco chagas,* the five wounds that Christ suffered on the cross… for each and every one of us. And finally, the seven castles on the perimeter of the shield represent the seven Moorish kings that were slain by Dom Afonso Henriques, the first… the first…

MAN
…the first King of Portugal! (*Exits with flag.*)

Lighting shift. CONCEIÇÃO *arrives home after school.*

VOICE OF CONCEIÇÃO'S FATHER
Good, Child, you are finally home.

CONCEIÇÃO
Pai. We must speak.

LUÍS *enters and takes* CONCEIÇÃO'S *hand.*

Voice of Conceição's Father
I am happy, Sãozinha, *querida.* You have made me happy.

Conceição
(*To audience.*) He was happy.

Lighting shift. This is now **Luís** *and* **Conceição's** *wedding.* **Man** *enters as* **Padre Madeira.** **Luís** *walks over to* **Him.** **Natália** *enters and helps* **Conceição** *put on her veil.* **Alexandre** *enters wearing military garb.* **Conceição** *is surprised to see* **Him.** **Natália** *leads* **Conceição** *to* **Luís.** **They** *all kneel before* **Padre Madeira.**

43

Padre Madeira
(*Quoting the Epistle of Paul to the Ephesians from memory.*) 'Wives, be in subjection unto your own husbands, as unto the Lord. For the husband is the head of the wife, as Christ also is the head of the Church, being himself the Savior of the Body. But as the Church is subject unto Christ, so let wives also be to their husbands in everything.'

Conceição *and* **Luís** *rise and hold hands.* **Padre Madeira** *continues, as* **They** *walk off together.* **Natália** *exits, but* **Alexandre** *remains with* **Padre Madeira,** *listening attentively.* **Conceição** *and* **Luís** *embrace.*

Padre Madeira
(*Overlapping with above action.*) 'Husbands, love your wives, even as Christ also loved the Church, and gave himself up for it; that he might sanctify it, having cleansed it by the washing of water with the word, that he might present it to himself a glorious Church, not having spot or wrinkle or any such thing; but that it should be holy and without blemish. Even so ought husbands also to love their wives as they do their own bodies.'

Conceição *laughs.* **Padre Madeira** *continues.*

Luís
I cannot believe you giggled during the reading! Are you a woman or a child?

CONCEIÇÃO
Let's find out.

LUÍS
What will I do with you?

CONCEIÇÃO
I'll give you a list.

PADRE MADEIRA
(*Continuing.*) 'He that loveth his own wife loveth himself: for no man ever hated his own flesh; but nourisheth and cherisheth it, even as Christ also the Church; because we are members of his Body. For this cause shall a man leave his father and mother, and shall cleave to his wife; and the twain shall become one flesh.'

CONCEIÇÃO
Tell me this is only the beginning. Tell me that my life has just started.

LUÍS
It has.

CONCEIÇÃO
Really?

LUÍS
Really. We are going to America.

CONCEIÇÃO *is about to react when all lights switch off except one spot on* PADRE MADEIRA.

PADRE MADEIRA
(*Concluding.*) 'This mystery is great: but I speak in regard of Christ and of the Church.'

Black out.
END OF ACT ONE

ACT TWO

Lights come up on the tableau from the end of Act One, with the addition of MANUEL *standing center stage.* CONCEIÇÃO *and* LUÍS *are in an embrace.* ALEXANDRE *is kneeling before* MAN *as* PADRE MADEIRA.

MANUEL
(*Shielding his eyes.*) Ma. Please.

CONCEIÇÃO *turns to* MANUEL. LUÍS *exits.* MANUEL *walks over to* ALEXANDRE *and* PADRE MADEIRA.

MANUEL   47
What happened here?

CONCEIÇÃO
Alexandre asked Padre Madeira to recommend him to the seminary. It was the only way for him to avoid being sent to Africa.

PADRE MADEIRA
Never. You will never be a man of God. And I pray the Army knows what it is getting.

MANUEL
Woah.

ALEXANDRE *and* PADRE MADEIRA *exit.*

MANUEL
(*Pause.*) How...?

CONCEIÇÃO
Hm?

MANUEL
How is it that I know this story, and yet don't know it, at the same time? (MANUEL *and* CONCEIÇÃO *share a moment. Pause.*) Did you move to the U.S. right away?

CONCEIÇÃO
It took a couple of years to scrape together enough money. Your father was working as a clerk at the police station in Ponta Delgada. He didn't like it very much. My father had arranged that position for him. He liked that even less. And I kept teaching, of course. (*Pause.*) Sit down. There's more.

MANUEL *rejoins the audience, which* CONCEIÇÃO *once again addresses.*

48

CONCEIÇÃO
Luís was very eager to move to America. He'd tell me how much opportunity we would find here—to make money, to be comfortable, to give our children everything. Luís wanted a big family. (*Pause.*) Actually, Luís scared me quite a bit.

LUÍS *enters.*

LUÍS
It is the truth. With Salazar incapacitated, and Caetano in charge, the revolutionary movement has grown even stronger. The harmless murmurs that I heard while I was on the mainland have become deafening cries for freedom from the dictatorship. A military coup is imminent. And once the government is overthrown, what of the Açores? What will stop us from declaring independence and descending into anarchy? São Miguel is no place to start a family.

CONCEIÇÃO
But isn't the United States at war?

LUÍS
That conflict is half a world away! It will not touch us. I promise you. (*Exit.*)

CONCEIÇÃO
All that really mattered to me was that I would be reunited with my sister.

MAN *carries on some luggage and exits.* CONCEIÇÃO *unpacks a few books.*
NATÁLIA *enters, carrying some dresses and a make-up bag.* SHE *looks older
now.*

CONCEIÇÃO
We've been living out of our suitcases for about two weeks now, down
here in Madrinha's basement.

NATÁLIA
(*To the audience.*) A Portuguese basement isn't like an American basement, even if it is in America. There is an unspoken agreement among
all Luso-Americans that using a cellar just for storage is immorally inef-
ficient. So, Joe's fixed it all up. We have a bedroom down here with heat
you can control, and a small bathroom. It's nice. And there's the play-
room on the other side with the ping-pong table for the boys, and Joe's
bar.

49

CONCEIÇÃO
Oh, I didn't say—Madrinha has two sons and a daughter now! All of
them are just beautiful!

NATÁLIA
We're waiting for the family that lives on the second floor to move
out—they will soon—and then Luís and Sãozinha can move in up
there.

CONCEIÇÃO
Those people on the second floor, they're such a nice couple. They also
moved to New Bedford from São Miguel, five years ago. They have
their second baby on the way, and they're moving into their own house
now. The woman, Dona Isabel, says it is beautiful. It's in a very quiet
area with lots of other big beautiful houses, right near a hospital. She
started to cry when she described it all to me. I cried with her.

NATÁLIA
She's crying because I won't be around to babysit her kids anymore.

Lighting shift. New Bedford. 1971.

NATÁLIA
Oh, my little Sãozinha, I still can't believe you're here with me! We haven't had one minute to ourselves since you moved in. But now that you've settled in and we've found Luís a job, you're all mine this afternoon! My Lord, you have become quite a woman! I'm glad I moved away before you bloomed!

CONCEIÇÃO
Madrinha!

NATÁLIA
Oh, please, Sãozinha, we're both grown women now. I insist that you start calling me Natália, like the rest of the world. (*Beat.*) Well, I'd better make sure Joe doesn't suddenly start sleep-walking.

CONCEIÇÃO
Stop it!

NATÁLIA
I'm just teasing you, My Little Sister.

CONCEIÇÃO
You call José 'Joe' like the Americans?

NATÁLIA
That's what all his friends call him, all the people at work. It stuck, what can I tell you? Once he started calling himself Joe, what was I to say, you know? I'm just lucky I have a name they can handle, or I'd be 'Natty' by now.

CONCEIÇÃO
Natty! (*Laughs. Pause.*) Oh no! What about me?

NATÁLIA
Ai yai yai. This will be a challenge. Maybe you should just stick with

'Maria.'

CONCEIÇÃO
No. No! 'Maria'! Everyone's Maria!

NATÁLIA
Not here.

CONCEIÇÃO
Still, I don't like it. No one has ever called me 'Maria da Conceição.'
What's wrong with just 'São'?   *51*

NATÁLIA
Easier than 'Conceição', that's for sure. Sãozinha. São. Sue? Suzie!

CONCEIÇÃO
'Suzie'? That doesn't sound like me at all.

NATÁLIA
OK, well, don't worry about it, honey. It will all figure itself out. And
anyway, I've got some exciting news.

CONCEIÇÃO
What? What is it?

NATÁLIA
They've just built a big mall up in North Dartmouth. (*Beat.*) And we're
going. (*Beat.*) Today.

CONCEIÇÃO
What's a mall?

NATÁLIA
Stores. Lots of stores. (*Beat.*) Like downtown? Only air-conditioned.

CONCEIÇÃO
That sounds wonderful, of course, but you said that you would help me

find some work today. Luís and I need the money. You said maybe the factory you used to work for, sewing the pockets…

NATÁLIA
Sãozinha, you just got here!

CONCEIÇÃO
I know, but… Luís is right. We need to make money. We are going to pay you all the rent that we can't pay you now! Luís will insist on that! And I want to start school here as soon as possible. You said we would get the information on the night school…

NATÁLIA
São! São! Shhhhh. Don't worry. You know I will help you. I just want to spend some time with you first. The kids are all at school and sometimes it gets… a little lonely around here. You'll let me show you around today, won't you? Oh, I knew you'd want to do this. I'm so excited. We're going to have so much fun together, aren't we? Now, pick out one of these outfits. And then sit at the mirror, we're going to fix you up nice for our outing. Come on.

CONCEIÇÃO
Aaaah, these skirts are… short.

NATÁLIA
Hey, we're in the nineteen-seventies now! You'll look so cute in… Oh. Oh, wait a second. You haven't shaved your legs above the knee yet have you? Oh, I'm sorry, no, no, that's OK, really. We'll take care of that later. No, no, what you have on is fine. Really. You'll be wearing your coat, anyway. Here, sit down.

CONCEIÇÃO
What kind of place is this? It's very fancy?

NATÁLIA
Oh, no, no. We're just dressing-up-to-go-out a little. How about some make-up, huh? Let me show you…

CONCEIÇÃO
I've never painted my face! Not even for the wedding!

NATÁLIA
Just a little.

CONCEIÇÃO
(*Pause.*) If you think I should. But not as much as yours.

NATÁLIA
(*Pause.*) Ooook. (*Pause.*) Look up. Ok. Hmmmmm…this should look
nice. Sit still. My Lord, maybe you haven't changed all that much. Ok,
look at me. Ok, go like this. Now you can look in the mirror.

53

CONCEIÇÃO
I don't know about this.

NATÁLIA
Oh, you look great! I'm so jealous, really. Now, don't let this upset you,
but the hair on your lip? No problem. Senhora Gonçalves down the
street, she does electrolysis, works wonders. See? She's great. (*Pause.*)
Wow, wait until Luís gets home and…

CONCEIÇÃO
No! Luís can't see me like this. He wouldn't approve.

NATÁLIA
Oh, come on. He's your husband, not your father, ok? This is America.
And, believe me, he's a man. He'll like it.

CONCEIÇÃO
José… Joe likes it?

NATÁLIA
Yes, Joe likes it. (*Pause.* **THEY** *both start to laugh.*) What?

CONCEIÇÃO
What? (**THEY** *both laugh again.*)

NATÁLIA
Listen, I'm going upstairs to get changed. Meet me up there when you're ready to go.

CONCEIÇÃO
Natália? Are you… are you happy? Does Joe make you happy?

54

NATÁLIA
Well, yeah. I mean, there are times… (*Beat.*) When he doesn't make me happy, I make me happy.

CONCEIÇÃO
And… the lovemaking?

NATÁLIA
That's what I was talking about.

CONCEIÇÃO
Oh, my. (**THEY** *both laugh. Pause.* **NATÁLIA** *starts to exit with the outfits.*)
Natália?

NATÁLIA
Yes?

CONCEIÇÃO
On the way back from your mall, we will go together to get that information on the night school, "OK?"

NATÁLIA
Sim, Conceição.

CONCEIÇÃO
Natália?

NATÁLIA
Yeeees?

CONCEIÇÃO
Nothing.

NATÁLIA
Nothing?

CONCEIÇÃO
Nothing.   *55*

CONCEIÇÃO *and* **NATÁLIA** *both sit down.* **THEY** *are now in different parts of the house. At first, their movements are identical, but as the following song continues, their movements diverge.* **LUÍS** *and* **MAN** *as* **JOSÉ** *enter. The song is directed at* **THEM**.

NATÁLIA
Rainbow circles through the screen door
Fill the kitchen that you built
A breeze is cutting through my hair
It lingers there
And then it plays like you just did

CONCEIÇÃO
'Hush now, don't you know they'll hear you?'
Moans that rumble up the walls
You tell me this is how you care
A little prayer
Just in case it's all untrue

NATÁLIA
I can smile when you touch me

CONCEIÇÃO
I can laugh when you tease me

NATÁLIA
I can jump into the shower when I know you're there

CONCEIÇÃO
I could always believe you

NATÁLIA
I could think you can please me

BOTH
Think I'll take it all with a Grain of Salt

NATÁLIA
A Grain of Salt that knows

CONCEIÇÃO
A Grain of Salt that grows

NATÁLIA
A Grain of Salt to choose

CONCEIÇÃO
A Grain of Salt to move

NATÁLIA
A Grain of Salt to hide my body

CONCEIÇÃO
A Grain of Salt in case I'm wicked

NATÁLIA
A Grain of Salt to stop his hunger

CONCEIÇÃO
A Grain of Salt to make it stronger.

The song stops abruptly. **LUÍS** *and* **JOSÉ** exit.

NATÁLIA
São, are you OK?

CONCEIÇÃO
Yes. Yes, Natália. I'll be right up.

NATÁLIA
Take your time.

CONCEIÇÃO
You too.   57

NATÁLIA exits.

CONCEIÇÃO
(*Walks over to her books.*) It's happening again. I have to find something to hold on to. Something that won't go away. Something that will keep me alive.

LUÍS *enters. Lighting shift. Ten months later. 1972.*

CONCEIÇÃO
Oh, thank God you're home. Come here. (*Pause.*) Luís? Come say hello.

LUÍS
Hello.

CONCEIÇÃO
Over here.

LUÍS
Conceição, please.

CONCEIÇÃO
What? What's wrong?

Luís
Nothing is wrong. I am tired. I have worked all day.

Conceição
How are your arms? (*Goes over to* **Luís**. *Pause. To audience.*) Luís said that his position was called a "shell-pusher." Now, you would think in a place like New Bedford, Massachusetts, that that would have something to do with seafood, but it didn't. Actually, the factory he worked for was producing munitions to send over to Vietnam. We never really talked about that, though. (*Back to* **Luís**.) Does that feel better? (*Pause.*) Oh, hey, good news. Dona Isabel tells me that we can move upstairs by next month! Finally, after almost a year down here. And, just in time, you know…

Luís
They think I am stupid.

Conceição
Who, Luís?

Luís
They think I am stupid. Because I do not understand their language.

Conceição
Oh, Luís, no…

Luís
Not that I can blame them, though. I stand there with that damn ignorant grin on my face whenever the supervisor decides to come over and yell at me. How am I to know what he is saying? *Eh, pá!* Even if I understood their English, what can I hear over the roar of those machines? I know what they call me. 'Portagee.' 'Greenhorn.' I know. But they know nothing. They are fools. I am the most educated man in that plant. 'A mathematical genius,' Padre Fernandes used to say. He said that to me. To my face. In front of all my classmates. I could be an accountant. Padre Fernandes said that. 'A mathematical genius,' he would say. Me! Now, I'm the Portagee.

58

CONCEIÇÃO

You are my husband. I know the sacrifices you are making for me—for our family. And I know how smart you are. Perhaps you could start going to school with me? The English is coming to me very quickly...

LUÍS

And who would pay for it? We have debts to repay! To my father, to your sister. I am working first-and second-shift, and it is barely enough for us to save anything at all!

CONCEIÇÃO   59

Luís, I will be able to teach here soon. Very soon. You will see. Everything will be fine.

LUÍS

We need money now. And I do not want to depend on my wife's paycheck.

CONCEIÇÃO

(*Pause.*) I need you to come sit down here with me.

LUÍS

My Lord, Woman, is that all you can think about? Have you not been listening? What more do you want from me? What is this demon that possesses you? Conceição—do not be infected by the rot and filth of this country. Do not watch the obscene television. Do not be seduced by the tramp your sister has become. If we are to survive in this country, if we are to win this battle for our lives, you need to be serious! Do you understand me? Listen to me. Listen to your husband. This vice is sinful, Conceição. I should not have to say such things to my own wife, but you leave me no choice. Is this all you want from me? This? This? Am I a man to you only in this regard? Is that what you think?

CONCEIÇÃO

(*Quietly.*) Luís. I am pregnant.

Luís
My Lord Jesus.

Conceição
(*Pause.*) Luís, please say something. (*Pause.*) I need you to say something. I need you, Luís.

Luís
(*In English, if necessary.*) *Pai nosso, que estais nos céus, santificado seja o vosso nome; venha a nós o vosso reino; seja feita a vossa vontade assim na terra como no céu. O pão nosso de cada dia nos dai hoje; perdoai-nos as nossas ofensas, assim como nós perdoamos a quem nos tem ofendido; e não nos deixeis cair em tentação; mas livrai-nos do mal.*

Conceição
(*During the prayer, to the audience.*) It seemed like every day after that, Luís became thinner and quieter. There were times when I could not remember the sound of his voice, the young man who once stood on my father's porch, looking out over the ocean for a land to conquer. (*Pause.*) After that night, we never made love again.

Luís
Amen. (*Exits.*)

Conceição
I stopped going to school during the pregnancy so that I could work more hours in the factory. I inspected fish fillets going by on a conveyor belt. I was too ashamed to continuously ask to go to the ladies' room, but the weight of that baby on my bladder... Well, let's just say that there were many days when my tears made those fish even saltier. (*Pause.*) Luís, too, worked every waking hour, despite the repercussions to his health. We told each other that we were preparing for our first child. In reality, we just couldn't face each other any longer. (*Pause.*) The birth of our son, Manuel Alexandre, brought some final moments of warmth and joy to our relationship.

Luís *enters holding a blanket.* **Luís** *carefully carries it over to*

Conceição, *who takes it.*

Conceição
Here was tangible evidence that we were in at least some ways carrying out the plans and dreams that Luís had laid out for our life in America. But nothing could change the fact that he had given up too much. They told me it was an accident.

Luís *lays down.* Conceição *covers him with the blanket.* Natália *enters.* Manuel *returns to the stage.*

61

Conceição
Oh God, no. Not this. Not again.

Manuel *steps into the action.*

Manuel
Ma, you don't have to do this.

Conceição
No, it's alright. Let me go on, Manuel. I'm alright. Please. We both need for me to finish this.

Conceição *leads* Manuel *back, giving* Him *to* Natália.

Conceição
Manuel was only six years old when his father died.

Natália, Manuel *and* Luís *exit. Lighting shift, focusing on* Conceição. *1979.*

Conceição
(*Pause.*) Oh, Ma-mãe, you didn't really have to come all this way. (*Beat.*) Yes, Pai, he was a good husband. He never once raised a hand to me, nor did he ever look at another woman. (*Beat.*) Yes, Mário, he had been ill for quite some time. (*Beat.*) Oh, Filipe, your little girl! She's so… (*Beat.*) No, Octávio. I'm fine. (*Beat.*) Yes. (*Beat.*) I will be. (*Beat.*) I

think so. (*Beat.*) Alright. (*Beat.*) Thank you.

A hand touches **Conceição's** *shoulder.* **She** *jumps. More lights come up. It is* **Alexandre**. **He** *is now a priest.*

Conceição
Oh, Alexandre! Thank God!

She *collapses into* **Alexandre's** *arms.* **He** *leads* **Her** *off a bit.* **They** *are now alone.*

Alexandre
Here. Come sit down, Suzie.

Conceição
Wait, the *rissóis*, I should…

Alexandre
They'll be fine. Natália will take care of everything downstairs. No one expects you to be in the kitchen. Not today.

Conceição
(*Breaking down.*) Oh God. Oh God. (**She** *lies down on the floor.*)

Alexandre
Shhhhh… quiet… it'll be OK.

Conceição
I can't believe he's gone. I think I just got used to him.

Alexandre
(*Carefully.*) You were married for ten years.

Conceição
That long? Are you sure? Wow, my life is just flying right by, isn't it?

ALEXANDRE
Are you alright? (*Sits down on the floor near* **CONCEIÇÃO**. *Pause.* **SHE** *begins to chuckle.*) Suzie? Suzie?

CONCEIÇÃO
Oh God, Alexandre, how could you have become a priest? (*Continues laughing.*)

ALEXANDRE
Why? Weren't you always impressed by my piety? (**CONCEIÇÃO** *laughs harder.*) Oh Lord, please, we shouldn't talk about this now. Not today. Not here. Please. I was just transferred to Immaculate Conception. (**CONCEIÇÃO** *laughs even harder.*) We'll have plenty of time for this later. You see, this is the reaction I thought I'd get when I first called you about going to the seminary. What did you say that day? 'This makes perfect sense.' Was that sarcasm? (**CONCEIÇÃO** *can only shake her head.* **ALEXANDRE** *starts to laugh, too.*) Hey, have you noticed that the men in your life tend to either come from or go to the seminary? This is a recurring theme for you. Have you considered the possibility that this is all your doing? (**THEY** *both laugh.* **ALEXANDRE** *recovers first.*) Do you want me to help you onto the bed?

CONCEIÇÃO
(*Between laughs.*) What kind of talk is that for a priest?

ALEXANDRE
Suzie!

CONCEIÇÃO
And with my husband dead for only four days!

ALEXANDRE
Shhh… please! They may hear you downstairs!

CONCEIÇÃO'S *laughs turn into sobs, and* **SHE** *begins to pound her fists on* **ALEXANDRE**.

ALEXANDRE
Suzie? Hey. Hey! Stop!

CONCEIÇÃO
How could you?

ALEXANDRE
What?

CONCEIÇÃO
How could you have left me?

ALEXANDRE
You don't want to have this conversation right now.

CONCEIÇÃO
How could you have left me?

ALEXANDRE
This isn't the time or the place to…

CONCEIÇÃO
How could you have left me?

ALEXANDRE
I didn't leave you, São. You left me.

CONCEIÇÃO's *and* **ALEXANDRE**'s *lines overlap in this next section.*

CONCEIÇÃO
What!? My life blows up around me…

ALEXANDRE
Your life, what about my life…

CONCEIÇÃO
Yes, my life. 'Good morning, you're getting married.' Does that sound

familiar?

ALEXANDRE
Well, how about 'Good morning, say good-bye to your one shot at a normal life.' Or how about 'Good morning, you're going to war.' It was an all-around bad day for me.

CONCEIÇÃO
A normal life!? You and me? Please explain to me how in your mind the two of us could have built a normal life with each other.

65

ALEXANDRE
OK, maybe not normal. But there was something real between the two of us.

CONCEIÇÃO
All I wanted was your friendship. That's all I've ever wanted.

ALEXANDRE
You were all I had to live for back then…

CONCEIÇÃO
Our relationship meant everything to me…

ALEXANDRE
…and then you were gone.

CONCEIÇÃO
…and then it was gone.

ALEXANDRE
(*Pause.*) You're right. I'm sorry. I had it all figured out in my head, and I never bothered to tell you about it, and when it started to fall apart…

CONCEIÇÃO
No, no. I'm sorry. I think maybe in my heart, I did know. And it scared me. How is it that I did know, and yet I didn't know, at the same time?

I'm not making any sense.

ALEXANDRE
Actually, I think I know exactly what you're saying. (*Pause.*) This isn't what I was expecting at all. When I heard about Luís, I thought I'd come by, let you know that I'd begun my novitiate here in the U.S., maybe say a blessing, lead a prayer…

CONCEIÇÃO
Things never seemed to go as planned with us, huh?

ALEXANDRE
Considering the last ten years of my life, that's not a joke.

CONCEIÇÃO
You and me both. (*Pause.*) What happened in Moçambique?

ALEXANDRE
It was war.

CONCEIÇÃO
What happened to you?

ALEXANDRE
I don't know what you want me to say. (*Pause.*) What is it you want to hear? That half the men I met over there were killed by land mines? That it didn't even feel like there was an enemy? The rebels would come over the border from Zambia just long enough to blow up a camp and plant some mines, and then they'd be gone, back over the border. We were fighting ghosts. We didn't stand a chance. And there was no honor in what we were doing there. Salazar had made certain that we'd all learned *"Deus, Pátria, Família"* all too well, but those people, the Africans, they were fighting for their homes. Their freedom. We were there because of Salazar's pride. He wanted his Empire. He wanted to be the Last Emperor. We were fighting for nothing. Sometimes, at night I would hear one of the men crying in the barracks, praying that he would be the next one to find a mine. And sometimes, it was me. (*Pause.*)

CONCEIÇÃO
I don't know what to say. I had no idea.

ALEXANDRE
Most people don't. That's the way it should be.

CONCEIÇÃO
You made it through.

ALEXANDRE
That's exactly what I did. I found a way through. God sent me an Angel
of Hope, São. He did.

67

MAN *enters as* **CHAPLAIN COSTA.**

ALEXANDRE
A chaplain arrived a few months after me. His name was Costa, too. He
had this one thing he would always say to us…

CHAPLAIN COSTA
There isn't always a way out, but God gives us a way through.

ALEXANDRE
I worked with him. Helped him to administer last rites. I got to know
him. And I learned that I wasn't alone. For the first time, I understood
who I was and what I was meant to do.

CHAPLAIN COSTA *exits.*

CONCEIÇÃO
I don't understand.

ALEXANDRE
I couldn't live my life alone, São. But you were the only girl I'd ever
cared for, the only one I could ever really speak to. I knew I wouldn't
get married. I couldn't. But without someone, without someone, I
couldn't make it through. So I did get married.

CONCEIÇÃO
Did I miss something!?

ALEXANDRE
I married Jesus Christ.

CONCEIÇÃO
Oh. Don't do that.

ALEXANDRE

I'm serious. It all made… so much sense. He's been very good to me.
(*Pause.*) When I finished up my two years of service, My Beloved
Chaplain recommended me to the seminary on Terceira, where he'd
graduated from. My father was ecstatic. He helped pay my way. Can
you believe that? My father. (*Pause.*) Look at us. You'd think we were
back in Covoada behind my father's henhouse.

CONCEIÇÃO
We are. Right now, we are. (**SHE** *puts her head in his lap, as in Act One.*)

ALEXANDRE
(*Pause.*) OK. Tell me. Now it's your turn. I remember this look in your
eyes. (*Beat.*) We can mourn for Luís together if that is…

CONCEIÇÃO
No, no! (*Pause.*) Father, forgive me, for I have sinned.

ALEXANDRE
Não, Sãozinha, not like this.

CONCEIÇÃO
Do it for me. You have to do this for me. I need it, Alexandre. Please.
(*Pause.*) Father, forgive me, for I have sinned. It has been… a long time
… since my last confession, and these are my sins. (*Pause.*) Father, my
husband died. And all I feel… is relief.

ALEXANDRE
São, don't say this!

CONCEIÇÃO
It's the truth. Luís was barely in the ground when I started thinking about going back to school. About teaching again. I know it's awful. I'm really an awful person. You don't know. I've become something horrible, Alexandre. Help me. Help me.

ALEXANDRE
What can I do? What do you want me to do?

69

CONCEIÇÃO
Talk to your husband. Find out what's happened. I have to know. There was some mistake. I'm wrong. Everything in me, everything about me, is wrong. The things I want. The things I want to do. All of it. Everything that's made me think I was alive. It's all been wrong.

ALEXANDRE
Querida. Shhhhh. Quiet. You just need some rest.

CONCEIÇÃO
No! I won't be quiet. Parts of me, all they are is evil. That's it. Why? Why would He do something like that? Is there some purpose? (*Beat.*) Am I a woman? Am I a woman? Yes? Why? Why would you think that? I was never the wife that Luís wanted. And I'm no mother. I'm ready to pack up and sneak out of this house right now. (*Beat.*) No. I won't. I won't leave Manuel. I won't let him become like me.

ALEXANDRE
Listen to me. Believe me. There isn't always a way out, but there is a way through. With the Grace of God, you have to keep looking straight ahead, push forward. Don't live in the past.

CONCEIÇÃO
I'm not in the past! This is all me!

MAN, NATÁLIA *and* LUÍS *enter.*

CONCEIÇÃO
All of it! Every moment! Every word I've been told! Every person who's touched me. Every heartbeat. It's all right here! Right now! (*Beat.*) It's all right here.

NATÁLIA, LUÍS *and* MAN *exit.*

CONCEIÇÃO
Give me my penance, Father.

ALEXANDRE
You've already done your penance, Child.

CONCEIÇÃO
No. No! (*Desperately.*) 'O my God, I am heartily sorry for having offended Thee, and I detest all my sins, because I dread the loss of heaven and the pains of hell, but most of all because they have offended Thee…'

ALEXANDRE
Suzie. Sãozinha. Look at me. I'm right here. You're not alone. 'God gives us a way through.' Hold on to me. I'm right here. (*Long pause.*)

THEY *kiss for a moment. Pause.* MANUEL *is heard from off-stage.*

VOICE OF MANUEL
What!? You kissed Father Alex!?

ALEXANDRE *exits.* MANUEL *enters.*

MANUEL
The Father Alex!? Our Father Alex!? My Confirmation godfather, Father Alex!? While my father's funeral reception was going on downstairs!? Now, ya know, I can't help but wonder whether he's helped raise me all these years just to make up for that. What about Tia Natália? Did you

have to kiss her too?

CONCEIÇÃO
Oh, hush, Manuel. It wasn't like that at all. (*Beat.*) And you've been very lucky to have godparents like yours. None of your American friends can claim to have had two sets of parents.

MANUEL
None of my friends want the one set they've got! (*Pause.*) Listen, Ma. I want you to know…I really am grateful for…

71

CONCEIÇÃO
No, no. That's not why I'm doing this. (*Beat.*) Manuel, do you remember the real story of how the island of São Miguel was discovered?

MANUEL
Well, yeah, I'd better. I think we covered that somewhere between Newton's Laws and Why You Don't Put the Cat in the Microwave—Not Even On 'Thaw.'

CONCEIÇÃO
Go ahead, then.

MANUEL
Me? (*Pause. To the audience.*) Well, as it turns out, Friar Gonçalo Velho did discover São Miguel, but not with any help from the Golden Light of Heaven. Actually, it was during one of the first missions carrying settlers to Santa Maria. While hunting down an escaped black slave, the Friar caught sight of São Miguel from a cliff. No one had noticed it before because, quite simply, São Miguel is only visible from Santa Maria under extremely clear weather conditions. (*Pause.*) Close?

CONCEIÇÃO
Close enough. I should let you go.

MANUEL
I… Yeah, I'd better… (*Begins to exit.*)

CONCEIÇÃO
If you'd like, I could clear my schedule and drive up with you tomorrow.

MANUEL
No, no. I know how busy you are this time of year, 'Professora Cordeiro.' UMass Dartmouth started classes two weeks before Boston College, what can you do? And I'd have to drive my car up there later anyway, so…

CONCEIÇÃO
Right.

MANUEL
But I'll see you on Family Weekend.

CONCEIÇÃO
And Alexandre, and Natália…

MANUEL
And my cousins, and their kids. And maybe their pets. You'll have to charter a bus, I'm sure. It'll be a full-blown Portagee stampede.

CONCEIÇÃO
You make fun, but they're proud of you. We're all proud of you. You're the smartest in the family.

MANUEL
No, I'm not. (*Begins to exit again. Stops.*) Mãe. I have no idea what I'm doing. (*Goes back over to* CONCEIÇÃO.) I need something to hold on to. Something that won't go away.

CONCEIÇÃO
(*To* MANUEL *and the audience.*) There is one word that is all ours. There is one word that cannot be touched by anyone else. The Americans try to call it 'nostalgia' or 'reminiscence' or 'yearning' or sometimes even 'melancholy.' But it's our secret. And with it, we have

the power to laugh and cry at the same time. *Saudade. Saudade. (Pause.)*
When I hear Ma-mãe, God rest her soul, singing in my head. *Saudade.*
When I walk halfway across the room and realize I have nowhere to go.
Saudade. At Christmastime, when I build the nativity scene with Pai's
old figurines and fresh moss and the little styrofoam sleigh that I made
my first year in America. *Saudade.* At night, when I touch my skin, and
I know sometimes something deep inside of me just wants to rip it all
off. *Saudade.* When I slowly whisper my whole name out loud—Maria
da Conceição Ferreira Amarelo Cordeiro. *Saudade.*

BOTH   73
Saudade.

CONCEIÇÃO *and* MANUEL *embrace.*

Blackout.

END OF PLAY

THROUGH A
PORTAGEE GATE

Patricia A. Thomas
(*Adapted from the memoir of the
same title by Charles Reis Felix.*)

For my parents, Margaret and Anthony Thomas,
who owned and operated their own business,
Thomas' Market, in New Bedford, Massachusetts.

"He is gone now. His shop is gone. Weld Square is gone. His life has been wiped clean off the board. But I wake in the night and I see his face and I hear his voice."

—Charles Reis Felix

Through a Portagee Gate was first performed as a staged reading on September 25, 2004, at the University of Massachusetts, Dartmouth, College of Visual and Performing Arts recital hall room 153. It was adapted from the memoir by Charles Reis Felix and directed by Patricia A. Thomas, and performed with the following ensemble:

Charles Reis Felix	David Splinter
Jose Felix	Richard Pacheco
Mother	Odete Amarelo
Jack	David Splinter
Podubnia/Mrs. Maud D'Haze	Trudi Miller

Through a Portagee Gate was developed to a full-length play at Culture*Park Theatre in New Bedford, Massachusetts, sponsored by the University of Massachusetts Dartmouth Center for Portuguese Studies & Culture. Adapted by Patricia A. Thomas, the play was performed at the University of Massachusetts Dartmouth Main Auditorium on April 29 and 30, 2006, with the following cast:

Francis A. Walker	William Hunter
Charles Reis Felix	Fred Cabral
Jose Felix	Richard Pacheco
Ilda	Nancy Leary
Charley	Kris O'Brien
Idalia/Radio Ensemble	Shannon Gracia
Harry Beech/Rezendes/	Ben Jolivet
Radio Ensemble	
Senhor Oliveira	João Ferreira
Podubnia/Radio Ensemble	Trudi Miller
Mrs. Maud D'Haze	Ann Flynn
Jack/Man	Vaughn Grae Dinsmore
Spanish Lady	Patricia A. Thomas

The play was directed by Patricia A. Thomas. The Production Manager and Designer was Rebecca Schade. The Stage Manager was Maurene Walker. Costume Design was by Niko Tarini. Original music for the Radio Ensemble was written by Patricia A. Thomas. Translation from the English to Portuguese was by João Ferreira.

Acknowledgments: to Richard Pacheco for his assistance in the development of the staged reading adaptation; to Rebecca Schade and Fred Cabral for their input and inspiration; to the staff at the WNBH

81

radio studio in downtown New Bedford; and to New York Shoe Repair on Dartmouth Street in New Bedford.

CHARACTERS

FRANCIS A. WALKER   *83*
President, Massachusetts Institute of Technology, 1893

CHARLES REIS FELIX
a writer and elementary school teacher, son of Jose and Ilda

HARRY BEECH
an elementary school teacher in Escamil, California

JOSE FELIX
a cobbler in New Bedford, Massachusetts, an immigrant from Setúbal,
Portugal.

SENHOR OLIVEIRA
a custodian in an elementary school in Escamil, California

ILDA
wife of Jose Felix

REZENDES
immigrant from Portugal, customer of Jose Felix

CHARLEY
young Charles, son of Jose and Ilda

IDALIA
sister of Charlie, daughter of Jose and Ilda

JACK
customer in Jose's shop

PODUBNIA
Polish-American customer in Jose's shop

MRS. MAUD D'HAZE
customer in Jose's shop, a Communist, and tenant of Jose's

SPANISH LADY

RADIO ENSEMBLE
(*played by members of the ensemble*)

MAN

ACT ONE

PROLOGUE

Lights up on a darkened auditorium setting. There is a podium in the cen-
ter of the stage, behind which the curtains are drawn.

FRANCIS A. WALKER

(*Enters through auditorium doors. Stands at microphone in front of closed curtains and addresses audience.*)
Good evening. Thank you for inviting me to speak. As President of
Massachusetts Institute of Technology, I will seize each and every
opportunity to give voice to the immigration dilemma that we now face
in this beloved country of ours. Let me be frank. So open, and broad,
and straight, now, is the channel by which immigration is being con-
ducted to our shores, there is no reason why every foul and stagnant
pool of population in Europe, from Ireland to the Ural Mountains,
should not be completely drained off into the United States. The stream
has fairly begun flowing and it will continue to flow so long as any difference of economic level remains; so long as the least reason appears for
the broken, the corrupt, the abject, to think that they might be better
off here than there. Taking whatever they can get in the way of wages,
living like swine, crowded into filthy tenement houses, piecing out their
miserable existence by systematic beggary at the doors of the rich and
by picking over the garbage barrels of our alleys, the arrival on our
shores of such masses of degraded peasantry brings the greatest danger
American labor has ever known. (**CHARLES** *appears onstage, focusing on*
WALKER. HE *walks toward him.* **WALKER** *disappears.*)

Lights up to reveal a classroom setting, stage right. There is a blackboard, desk and chair. This is **CHARLES REIS FELIX'S** *classroom in an elementary school in Escamil, California. It is 1971.*

(**HARRY BEECH**, *and* **CHARLES** *enter having just attended a faculty meeting.* **CHARLES** *is carrying a typewriter.*)

BEECH
Welcome to Escamil, Charles. This is your classroom. Remember, no tacks!

(*Laughing.*)

CHARLES
Only straight pins. What a meeting! Are all administrators like that? Bullshit flows in a never-ending stream.

BEECH
'Fraid so! Don't worry about him. No, you'll enjoy it. And I'm looking forward to working with you. These kids are good. For the most part. They're just ranch kids. They don't study much, but they're calm. They have a different rhythm. (**HE** *gestures.*) Not like city kids. (*Begins to exit.*)

CHARLES
Sure. (*Opens his typewriter case, and sets up typewriter on desk.*)

BEECH
(*Returning.*) Keep your fingers on the Mexican kids, though—they're lazy. You know how it is with them—everything is *mañana*. Slower than the Second Coming of Christ. (**THEY** *laugh together.*) Where are you from originally? Is that an Eastern accent I detect?

CHARLES
I guess so. A little place in Massachusetts.

BEECH

Oh. A Yankee! I thought so. You'll be fine! You have the experience. Listen, if something goes wrong, something's missing, remember "Cherchez le Mexicain." (*Exits. Returns, sticking his head back in classroom.*) Felix. Interesting. What kind of a name is it anyway?

CHARLES

It's a French name. It's pronounced "Fay-leaks" in French. (*Writes* **FAY-LEAKS** *on the board.*)

BEECH

89

Oh! Thought so. I love Paris. (*Exits*)

CHARLES

(*Alone in the classroom.*) Shit! (*Turns to board. Erases board. Writes* **CHARLES REIS FELIX** *on board. To himself.*) New Bedford. I'm from New Bedford, Massachusetts. I'm masquerading as an American. (*Sits at desk and rolls a piece of paper into typewriter.* **HE** *types.*)

JOSE

(**JOSE FELIX** *appears to* **CHARLES.**) You know, you shouldn't call yourself Charles. That's not your name. Your name is *Caarlessssh.* That is what it says on your birth certificate. Someday you're going to be sorry. It's going to cause you trouble. You're going to have a hard time proving who you are.

CHARLES

Pa! (*To himself.*) Caarlessssh. (*Resumes typing.*)

SENHOR OLIVEIRA

(*Enters classroom with mop and bucket. Looks at name on board. Looks at* **CHARLES** *who is busy typing.* **OLIVEIRA** *washes the board and exits.*)

CHARLES

(*Typing, then reading, and to audience.*)
I was brought up in the North End of New Bedford among Jickies,

Frogs, Polocks, and other Portagees, with a sprinkling of Jews for flavor. We were all foreigners or the children of foreigners, so we were all equals. There were strange smells coming from every kitchen. Nobody could lord it over anybody else.

(*At board,* **CHARLES** *draws a map with chalk.*) We lived on Coffin Avenue. My neighborhood extended from above Ashley Boulevard to the end of the street, to the Taber Mill and the New Bedford Cotton Mill. Coffin Avenue from Ashley Boulevard to North Front Street was almost solidly French. Below North Front Street to the Acushnet River, Coffin Avenue was Portuguese. I was glad that I did not live toward the bottom of Coffin Avenue. There they had big three-tenement houses all crowded together. The yards were narrow strips of dirt between houses. There were no flowers in the yards. In my neighborhood we had fewer people and more space, some cottages with two stories but just one family in them, some two-tenement houses like mine with big yards with grass, and flower-beds in every yard. My yard had lilac "trees," rose bushes, honeysuckle vines, everything so sweetly fragrant in the summertime. My father had a cobbler's shop at 868 Acushnet Avenue.

Lights up on **JOSE**'s *Cobbler Shop.* **JOSE** *appears on stage.*

His shop is gone. Wiped clean from the map. But I can still see his face and hear his voice.

JOSE
You never show what you are thinking, because if you show what you are thinking, they'll think, 'This is a dumb guy. Let's take his pants off!' They will try to attach the dog.

Light change center stage, as **JOSE** *and* **CHARLES** *meet together to look out at the street.*

CHARLES
(*Animated. Standing with* **JOSE**.) He loved to tell stories. Yesterday, or twenty years ago, it was all the same to him. Some of his stories were about funny things that happened in Weld Square, like the time the two bums conspired to victimize the butcher who ran the Kosher Meat

Market. One of the bums went in the alley behind the store and began banging loudly on the wall. The butcher, not knowing what was going on, went into his backroom to investigate the noise. The other bum, dashed into the store, grabbed a chicken that was hanging from a hook and dashed out.

JOSE
The butcher gave chase, running after him. 'Stop him! Stop him!' he cried. But nobody stopped him. The people were all laughing.

CHARLES   *91*
And so the two bums, working together, got themselves a chicken dinner. Another funny story was the apples bonanza. A big open truck with a load of loose apples passing through Weld Square swerved to avoid a car pulling away from the curb, and tipped over, spilling the apples all over the street. After the crash, there was a moment's silence and then seemingly by magic, a crowd of people suddenly materialized, all of them brandishing paper bags. How did they get there so fast? My father watched from his window.

Lights come up on the kitchen of the **FELIX** *family home.*

JOSE
I don't know where those people came from! (**ILDA, JOSE'S WIFE,** *enters kitchen.*) There was nobody there and then pfft! There they were. They all came running, old ladies, little kids, men, everybody. They bent over in the street and started filling their bags with the apples. The poor distraught truck driver tried to stop them. He grabbed an old lady's bag and tried to get it away from her, an old Polocka lady, but the Polockas are tough. She wrestled him for it, all the time screaming at him. But while he was doing that, all the others kept filling their bags. Finally he just gave up and watched them. That was all he could do. In the end, the people cleaned the street. They took everything, even the mashed apples. I guess they made applesauce out of them. You didn't need to call the street cleaners, so I guess in a way they saved the City some money.

CHARLES
But most of his stories were serious—battles over fifty cents, seventy-five cents, maybe a dollar.

JOSE
(*Entering kitchen, to* ILDA.) He tried to stick me for seventy-five cents, oh, yes he did.

ILDA
Did he pay?

JOSE
He paid.

CHARLEY *enters and sits at kitchen table.*

CHARLES
Once, the world of J.P. Morgan and Rockefeller came to him. Once he sat at the corporate table as a player.

JOSE
This happened in 1921. At the time I had a shop on Coggeshall Street. That was my first shop. Weld Square was my second shop. Have you ever heard of the Cities Service Company, Charley? They own gasoline stations not only here in New Bedford but all over the United States. They make the advertise on the radio. This is a tremendous company, very big, with great influence. Well, the Cities Service Company took it in their heads to build a gasoline station on Coggeshall Street. Why they picked that street I don't know. Nobody there owns a car.

IDALIA
They picked it because it's by the Coggeshall Bridge. All the people driving to Fairhaven and Cape Cod will pass their station.

JOSE
It was going to be big, very big, oh yes. But there was no space there for

a gasoline station. So their plan was to knock down all the buildings. So they bought the buildings and then kicked out all the people. I had them. I had a lease. With me there they could not build the gas station. They had to deal with me. This man in the suit and tie returned. 'Well what do you say, Joe?' I looked him in the eye and I said, 'Here is what I say to you! I don't go for three hundred dollars! I don't go for less than five hundred dollars!' 'All right, Joe,' he said, and he went over to the counter and he wrote out a check in my name for five hundred dollars. 'Joe,' he said to me, 'you drive a hard bargain.' Yes, that's what he said. 'Joe, you drive a hard bargain.' (*Laughs.*) Five hundred dollars! For doing nothing! Without lifting a finger! Easy money! Just for signing my name to a piece of paper. And they moved me free! Five hundred dollars! That was a good piece of work, a very good piece of work. Think of how many shoes I would have to fix to make five hundred dollars! (*Laughs. Then, confidentially, to audience.*) And I ended up in a better place than the place I left. I should have paid them instead of them paying me!

ILDA

I'm surprised you admit it. (*To audience.*) It was the best thing that ever happened to him. If they hadn't pushed him out of there, he never would have budged from that shop. He'd still be there today. But he didn't want to go to Weld Square. He was afraid to go there. He wanted to find another place on Coggeshall Street. It was me who talked him out of it.

JOSE

(*Smiles.*) They took me for a dumb greenhorn! But I showed them! I picked their pocket!

(**ILDA** *puts bread on table.* **CHARLEY** *sits at table.*)
This scoundrel... (*Takes a big bite out of a chunk of Portuguese bread*) This swindler... (*Chews some more thoughtfully.*) This accursed thief ... (*Another bite.*) This son of a whore... (*Chews some more.*)

ILDA

Get to the point, man! It takes you all day to tell a story! Either talk and don't eat, or eat and don't talk.

JOSE
This scoundrel came in my shop. (**REZENDES** *appears.* **HE** *is wearing a bowler hat.*) He was Portuguese, well-dressed, clean-shaven. He carried himself with a certain air. He had a big smile on his face like we were old friends. I had never seen him before.

REZENDES
O Senhor Mestre.

JOSE
…He said to me. Who is this? I was thinking. He doesn't even know me and he's calling me '*O Senhor Mestre.*'

ILDA
That's just a polite form of address. You have met so few well-brought-up people that you think he's making fun of you.

JOSE
Well, I was suspicious of him.

ILDA
Of course you were suspicious of him. You were suspicious because he wore clean clothes and talked respectfully to you. But if he had come in your shop and farted and spit on the floor and talked crudely, then you would have liked him. (*To* **CHARLEY.**) He is only comfortable with his own kind.

JOSE
Here she is. She hasn't met the man but she is giving me a lecture about him. She knows everything about him. This woman knows everything.

ILDA
Never mind. Go on with your story. It's just that somebody has to tell the truth.

JOSE

When a guy comes at you with elaborate politeness, watch out! He is up to something. He wants to attach the dog! Oh, yes! (**HE** *turns to* **REZENDES**.)

REZENDES

Sir Master, you are renowned throughout the North End—the North End?—I don't do you justice!—you are renowned throughout the whole city of New Bedford for your unequaled skill in repairing shoes. I was told by more than one—yes, I was told by more than one—there is a man who is a master of his craft. No one can compare to him in this whole city. The other shoemakers should apprentice to him! Yes! That's what I was told!

JOSE

(*To* **ILDA**.) He's looking at me, studying me, seeing if I'm lapping this shit up. He's setting the trap to get me.

REZENDES

There is no more accomplished shoemaker in the whole city, I was told. He can fix anything, they said to me. If it can be fixed, he can fix it. No job is too difficult for him.

JOSE

What does this clown want?

REZENDES

You know, there is nothing in America to compare with the majestic beauty of Portugal. We may be a poor country but we are rich in the physical beauty of our land and we are rich in the compassionate souls of our people. (**HE** *gives his shoes to* **JOSE** *for repair. Then…*) Awww.

JOSE

(*To audience. Laughing.*) What an actor! He should… he should… he should have been in the movies! (*To* **REZENDES**.) What's the matter?

95

REZENDES
O esteemed Sir Master. Can you help me? I have nowhere else to turn.

JOSE
What is it?

REZENDES
I have a heavy heart, Sir Master. A heavy, heavy heart. O my good
friend! (**HE** *is crying.*)

JOSE
Get hold of yourself, man.

REZENDES
It's my wife, my beloved wife. She is at death's door. Only an operation
can save her. And the Jew doctor won't operate unless he has a hundred
dollars in his hand beforehand. I don't know what to do! I don't have
the money! I don't know where to turn! Can you help me, Sir Master?

JOSE
He wants a hundred dollars from me. Me, a perfect stranger to him. He
wants a hundred dollars!

REZENDES
My valued friend. You are Portuguese, so I know you have the heart of a
Portuguese. I wouldn't ask you if you were French or English or Polish;
I'd know I'd be wasting my time. But you are Portuguese. You have the
soul of a Portuguese. (*Crying.*) A life depends on you, Sir Master. And if
you save her, I will bless you till the day I die. And my wife and all my
children will bless you. And you will not lose a penny. I will pay you
back two hundred dollars! I swear it on my faith as a Catholic! Can you
do it, Sir Master? Can you lend me the hundred dollars? Can you save
my wife?

JOSE
All right, I'll give him one right back. (*To* **REZENDES**.) Respected coun-
tryman, I am just a poor cobbler. I have twelve hungry children waiting

for me at home.

ILDA
Liar! (*In Portuguese.*) Such a liar! He has no shame!

JOSE
As much as I would like to help you, my first duty is to them. I cannot deprive them of food. My conscience would not permit me.

REZENDES
Well, can you give me anything to save my wife? Five dollars. Ten dollars. Anything? I will be eternally grateful.

97

JOSE
I cannot give you a cent. You cannot ask a man to starve his own children.

ILDA
Liar! Such a liar!

JOSE
He knew he wasn't going to attach the dog then. His expression changed. (**REZENDES** *exits.*) No more 'Sir Master' stuff!

ILDA
And how do you know he wasn't telling the truth?

JOSE
Because he was full of shit, that's how come. I wanted to find out about the guy. He told me he lived on Earle Street near the Portuguese Church. I have a customer who lives on Earle Street near the Church, and he works at the *Ahm-ah-sah-ree-us*. So I asked him, 'Do you know this fellow who lives near the Portuguese Church by the name of Rezendes?' 'I know that guy,' he said. 'He's always complaining about America, that you can't enjoy life here because you have to work too hard, and he's always talking about the beauties of Portugal. He left for Portugal on Saturday and he's gone to stay.' 'What about his wife? I

asked. Did she go with him?' 'What wife? He has no wife.' So he swore on his faith as a good Catholic. I'm sure he goes to church every Sunday. It was all a trick to rob me. (*To* CHARLEY.) It is necessary to be very careful in this life. You have to remember that. There are people for everything in this world.

CHARLES'S *classroom in Escamil, California.*

CHARLES
(CHARLES *in classroom, at board. 1930s music playing under. Writes 'Attaching the Dog' on the board. Speaking to audience.*)
There weren't too many dogs running around the North End of New Bedford in the 1930s. Dogs eat food. Food costs money. And there was no money to spare. Dogs were simply a luxury people could not afford. The lack of dogs in the North End might partly explain the strong reaction to them at the Portuguese church on Earle Street one balmy Sunday at 12 noon. Two dogs were cavorting on the steps of the church just as the eleven o'clock Mass let out.

CHURCH-GOERS *come out of the church and step around the dogs. The* MEN *turn away and leave the* WOMEN *on stage.*

LADY # 1
(*Shielding* HER *eyes.*) Don't look!

LADY #2
It's intolerable! They come here on the church steps to do their business! I wish I had a pan of hot water!

LADY #3
Aarrrgghhh!

CHARLES
These two sacrilegious dogs were engaged in a sexual act. The male dog was, in a manner of speaking, physically attached to the female. The male dog was screwing the female. From this observation came the Portuguese expression, "attaching the dog." It means to screw someone

figuratively, to victimize him, to cheat him, to make a fool of him. The Portuguese are a fastidious people when it comes to sexual matters. They have a great delicacy in these things. I suspect there is no such word as "screwing" in the Portuguese language. If there is, I never heard it. My father never said, 'He screwed me,' he would say, 'He attached the dog.' It was one of my father's favorite expressions. Dog attachings or attempted dog attachings were at the heart of many of his stories. In the never-ending war with his customers, someone was always trying to attach the dog to him. Sometimes the person succeeded, and then there was no joy in Mudville that day.

JOSE
(*Out on the street.*) He attached the dog. Yes. He attached the dog. He did a good one on me. Yes, he did. That son of a whore. (*Spits.*) He stick me for seventy-five cents. (**JOSE** *crosses to shop.*)

PEOPLE *appear on the street, in front of the shop.*

CHARLES
Every man in business is different. Sam Genensky, who ran a pawn shop a few doors down from my father never made small talk with the customers. My father was different. He liked to chat. He kept his finger on the economic pulse of the city. He knew which mills were laying-off and which mills were working.

JOSE
(*To* **WOMAN** *passing by.*) You working? (*To another.*) Busy?

MAN
Slack.

JOSE
(*To someone else.*) So, his father threw him out?

CHARLES
He knew stuff that was happening on our street even before my mother did.

ILDA
(*From kitchen.*) How do you know that?

JOSE
Never mind how I know. (*Sly smile.*) I know, that's all. (**JOSE** *and* **CHARLEY** *enter shop.*)

ILDA
He's worse than an old woman. Down there in that shop, gossiping.

100   *Lights up full on cobbler shop.* **CHARLEY** *and* **JOSE** *are working in shop.* **JACK** *enters.*

JOSE
Jack!

JACK
Hey Joe. (*Reading the newspaper. After a while.*) You know this fellow they're investigating in Boston, the friend of the Mayor's, what's his name now? Boyle, Edward Boyle.

JOSE
Yes. What did he do?

JACK
Well, they're saying now that he overcharged the City of Boston one million dollars for that building he built.

JOSE
One million dollars!

JACK
Yes, one million dollars, Joe. And that's not all. One of the inspectors went over to the foundation of that building, it's supposed to be concrete, you know, and it's such good quality concrete the inspector said he scratched it with his fingernail and it began to crumble.

JOSE

He scratched it with his finger and it began to fall apart!

JACK

Yes, the concrete began to crumble. You see, what he did, what Boyle did, was this—to save money he didn't put enough cement in the concrete. Say that he was supposed to put in five sacks of cement in a batch, why then he'd put in two sacks. That way the concrete is mostly sand and that's why it crumbles.

JOSE

He was supposed to put in five sacks of cement, but he'd put in two and charge the City for ten!

JACK

Now they're looking for the inspector who passed on that building. And the building is only five years old.

JOSE

Only five years old!

JACK

Yes, only five years old. They had to move the people, all those offices out of the building. It's been condemned as unsafe.

JOSE

What crooks. The State should pass a law. The Irish can't run for office. It would save a lot of money. Watch out! Here come the Irish! Such crooks! They steal with both hands! They steal and then they go see the Pope! (*Resumes working. After a while...*)
What number came out yesterday?

JACK

Three-six-five.

JOSE

I played seven-two-eight. Didn't even get one of them right. What looks good today, Jack?

JACK
Well, I'll tell you, Joe. This truck came by yesterday and I noticed his number plate: nine-oh-two. I didn't think anything of it at the time, but this morning I asked Freddie what time it was and he said, 'Nine-oh-two.' I think somebody is trying to tell me something, Joe. I'm going to play that number today and I'm gonna play it heavy. I'm going to put a quarter on it.

JOSE
Whew! That'll be a hundred twenty-five dollars if you win! I like that number but I can't use it, it's yours. I like my shop number — 868. 868 Acushnet Avenue. I'm gonna play 868, Jack. (**THEY** *study the numbers.* **JACK** *reads newspaper.* **JOSE** *walks to door and looks out.*)

Lights up in front of shop. The following is seen through **JOSE**'s *eyes, as he looks out onto the street.*

JOSE (*cont.*)
Oh, shit! Here comes that Frenchman, Thibodeau! (*Hiding shoe.*) I know this guy. If he sees me working on his shoes, he will stay and watch me. He's fussy like an old woman. I'll have him here breathing down my neck, asking me questions, and telling me what to do. There won't be any getting rid of him.
(*Looking some more.*) Look! Look! See that fellow there? (*Pointing to a guy walking by.*) That's Kid Curly, the Portagee rassler! He fights at the Bristol Arena! He comes in here to get his shoes fixed! Yes, he does! That poor devil Curly. He's young, but he has four kids. He's on WPA!
(*Seeing a* **RABBI** *walk by.*) Look! Look at those whiskers! You can't even see his face! I think it's against their religion for him to shave. The ordinary people can, but the rabbi can't. Maybe he's going over to the butcher of the Jews to inspect the meat. Jews won't eat the meat, you know, unless it's stamped by the rabbi. That's good for the rabbi. That way he can earn a little money. I'm sure he doesn't do that for free.
(*A* **MAN** *hurries by the shop, carrying a small radio.*)
Look at that Polock! He is in a rush to get to the pawnshop. I see that

guy come by here many times bringing things to Sam. One time he came by with a set of dishes!

Lights shift.

Hey, hey! The other day this bum entered in the store of the butcher of the Jews and asked him, 'How much are your pork chops?' The butcher showed him a face very long. 'We don't carry pork chops,' he said. It was an insult to his religion, you see. The bum didn't have any money. He just did that for a joke!

103

Lights out, then up inside radio station, WNBH, *in downtown New Bedford. Those in cobbler shop listen to radio.*

RADIO ENSEMBLE
(*Enter to microphone.Singing.*) W-N-B-H
(*Reading from radio script.*) This comedy moment brought to you by 'Duz.' 'Duz does it all!'

(**ENSEMBLE** *take turns telling jokes.* **THEY** *accompany themselves using objects and instruments to achieve sound effects that punctuate each joke.*)

Knock, knock!
Who's there?
Cash.
Cash who?
I knew you were a nut!

Knock, knock!
Who's there?
Lydia.
Lydia who?
The lid a ya trash can just blew off!

Knock, knock!
Who's there?
General Lee.

General Lee who?
General Lee I do not tell jokes…

Knock, knock!
Who's there?
Doughnut.
Doughnut who?
(*With accent.*) Doughnot ask me again!

Knock knock!
Who's there?
Dewey.
Dewey who?
Dewey have to listen to all this knocking?
(*Sound effects, and* **ALL EXIT**. *Lights bump out.*)

Spotlight searches auditorium as **CHARLES** *takes the stage, a-la-stand-up-comedy-act, for the following monologue. We hear a laugh track from time to time.*

CHARLES
(*As a stand-up comic.*) In New Bedford, in the 1930s, the Portuguese were called Portagees. This was the universal word for Portuguese in New Bedford. Even the Portuguese used it when they spoke English. It was both a noun and adjective. 'He's a Portagee.' 'He speaks Portagee.' 'He eats Portagee bread.'
(*Pause for laugh-track.*)
   The Polish were called Polocks. 'He's a Polock.' 'He speaks Polock.' 'He goes to the Polock church.' The English were called Jickies, as in, 'He's a Jickie.' I have no idea where this word came from or what it meant. I have heard it only in New Bedford and only back then. A variation of it was Jick, as in, 'He's a Jick.' The French were called Frogs. I presume this came from Napoleonic days when the English referred to their French foes as Frog Eaters. This was the height of arrogance: to eat English food and to make derogatory comments about anyone else's cuisine. And in New Bedford I saw no evidence of the supposed French affinity for amphibian fare. The Jews were called Jews.

Sometimes an adjective was added. For the French, the adjective was the alliterative 'fuckin'. 'That fuckin Frog,' or, 'That fuckin Frenchman.' For the Portuguese, it was 'dumb.' 'That dumb Portagee,' or, more personally, 'You dumb Portagee!' many times that I had periods of doubting my own smartness. Could they be right? Were all Portagees dumb? And after a while, the 'dumb' seemed less like an adjective and more like a noun. Because if you said, 'That dumb Portagee,' it sounded like this specific Portagee was dumb but the possibility existed that other Portagees were not. But if it began to sound like there was no discrimination involved, then it came out, 'That Dumb Portagee,' like 'Dumb' was part of a compound noun and was affixed permanently to 'Portagee.'

105

For the Polish, it was 'square-headed.' 'That square-headed Polock.' I saw a TV drama featuring an American-born insurance investigator of Polish extraction. He was introduced to a man and the man said, 'That's a Polock name, isn't it?' Our hero instantly clocked the lout with one punch. If our hero had been in the North End of New Bedford in the Thirties, he would have quickly become arm weary. You would have had to pick your way carefully through the streets so as not to step on the fallen bodies.

For the Jews, it was 'goddamn.' 'That goddamn Jew.' (*Pause.*) What you never heard was, 'That dumb Jew.'

The Jewish kids in the North End did not fight. Everyone understood that, so they were not challenged. I wished everybody else was like that. Among the other nationalities, you could never totally relax. The Jewish boys could be seen after school trudging through the streets on their way to a violin lesson. This was a totally familiar and unremarkable sight. Jewish boys played the violin. That was to be expected. On the other hand, if a Polish boy had been seen in the streets carrying a violin case to a lesson, heads would have turned and he would have been stared at. Women would have stuck their heads out of windows and shouted down to their neighbor, 'Look, Mabel! There goes a Polock kid with a violin!!!' (**CHARLES** *exits. Spotlight out.*)

Sound of Jewish violin music. Lights full on shop as **PODUBNIA** *enters.*

JOSE
(*Speaking to her tenderly.*) Hello, Podubnia! How you feelin', Podubnia?

PODUBNIA
I'm tired, Joe. Awfully tired. (**SHE** *sits.*)

JOSE
You gettin' old, Podubnia.

PODUBNIA
I don't know. I think it's the work.

JOSE
You still working at the same place?

PODUBNIA
Yes. At the Firestone.

JOSE
You been there a long time. They running good?

PODUBNIA
Very good. We got two shifts going now. They need cord for the tires. (**SHE** *hands* **JOSE** *her shoes.*)

JOSE
(*Taking shoes.*) Tappees, Podubnia?

PODUBNIA
Yes.

JOSE
I think the heels are still all right. I'll just do the tappees. When you want them, Podubnia? Friday all right?

PODUBNIA
There's no rush, Joe. Any time is all right.

JOSE
I'll have them for you Friday.

PODUBNIA
(*With a groan* **SHE** *gets to her feet.*) I think it was better in the old days, Joe. Longer hours but less machines. Work more hours but more slow. I like that better. Today they give you too many machines. (*Demonstrating.*) I have to run to keep up. You can't stop for nothing.

JOSE
(*Sympathetically.*) I know how that is. Everything today is getting like that. Customers want their shoes right away. Nobody wants to wait.

107

PODUBNIA
They give you too much. Too many machines for one person to take care of. Have to run around like crazy people. Too much speedup, Joe! Too fast, too fast! (**SHE** *exits and freezes outside of the shop door, as Jose tells the following story.*)

JOSE
Take care of yourself, Podubnia. (**JOSE** *turns to* **CHARLEY** *and* **JACK**.) That woman was arrested during the big strike. She threw a brick through a window of the mill. They gave her thirty days in jail. New Bedford had a big strike once. You were just a little boy then. The mills were going to cut the pays so all the workers went on strike. All the mills close down. She was working at the Ahm-ah-sahree-us then. She was on—how do you call it?—the picket line. And she picked up a brick and threw it and broke a window. The mill called the police and they sent Cop Hickey. And when Cop Hickey tried to arrest her, she hit him over the head with her umbrella. Cop Hickey had to call for help. (**ALL** *laugh together at the image.*)

JOSE *and* **CHARLEY** *resume working on shoes. We hear the rhythmic pounding.* **JACK** *reads the newspaper.*

JACK
(*After a while…*) Hey, I was there the night Goulart died, Joe.

JOSE
You were there?

JACK
Yes, I was there. Goulart jumped on the table and he said, 'As your Representative in Boston, I'm going to do this. I'm going to do that.' He was full of promises. And then he dropped dead right in the middle of his speech. The Portagees are going to have to elect somebody else. (*Reading some more.*) You know the manager of the A&P store, Joe? That French guy?

108

JOSE
Yes, I know who he is.

JACK
Well, he got fired Saturday night.

JOSE
Is that right?

JACK
Yes. One of the big shots came down from Boston, walked in the store about six o'clock, and said to him, 'You're all through here.' Took his keys from him and sent him home. Took about five minutes. And he worked for them twenty-two years.

JOSE
That man looks to be in his fifties. How is a man that old gonna get another job today?

JACK
He's forty-two, Joe.

JOSE
He looks like he's in his fifties.

JACK
No, he's forty-two, Joe.

JOSE
I think they made a mistake firing him. That man is a hard worker. I've seen him in there night after night when I go home. The store is closed but he's in there all by himself, working.

JACK
Well, it didn't do him any good, Joe. The company warned him six months ago. They told him to make more business at that location. But I don't know what he could have done about it. The prices at that store are too high for this neighborhood. He put in a clerk who can speak Portagee. He put in another clerk who speaks French. He put in another clerk who speaks Polish. But it didn't do any good. The people like to talk their own language, but they want low prices. He was with them twenty-two years. Worked his way up to be manager. Never worked for anybody else. I know what happened, Joe. When you've worked a long time for somebody, they get tired of having you around. They get tired of looking at you, so they fire you.

109

JOSE
You and me are smart, Jack. We work for ourselves. We don't work for a boss. Shit on the boss!

JACK
Yeah. We work for the public, so everybody's our boss! (**JACK** *exits.* **CHARLEY** *runs home.*)

JOSE *listens to the radio as he closes up the shop. Lights up on radio station.*

RADIO ENSEMBLE
(*Enter to studio platform. Singing.*) W-N-B-H, New Bedford…

BEN
(*Reading from radio script.*) This today… Nearly 30,000 textile mill workers in New Bedford are on strike. Scarcely any workers entered the

mills the first day of the strike. A sense of celebration marked the informal pickets at the mill gates; strikers wore their best clothes and brought picnic breakfasts. New Bedford movie theatre managers are reporting record crowds at the matinees. People who have been working in the mills since the age of twelve and thirteen say the strike brings a welcome change in routine. The Textile Mill Committee is demanding a twenty percent increase in wages, a forty-hour workweek, equal pay for equal work, an end to child labor, and no retribution against union members.

110

SHANNON
(*Reading.*) Hey listeners! Try to stay positive! Here are two products that make people smile. Remember, *Ipana* toothpaste for the 'smile of beauty,' and *Sal Hepatica* for the 'smile of health!' (*Reading from script.*) 'What a fool she is! She caught cold on her honeymoon!' Professional opinion says it didn't have to happen. Bristol-Myers is there for you! Remember…smile…
(ENSEMBLE *exit.*)

JOSE
(JOSE *walks home and enters kitchen.* CHARLEY *is sitting at the table.* JOSE *takes* CHARLEY'S *hand.*) Come on, Charley. Come on with me. We're going to have some fun. We're going to count some money! Shhh. Let's go up to the attic. Nobody will bother us!
(THEY *walk up the stairs to the attic.*)

CHARLEY
(*Putting his hand up to the ceiling.*) I like the slant of the ceiling! (THEY *circle around climbing the attic stairs.*)

JOSE
(HE *locks the door and tests it.*) Sit down, Charley. (JOSE *sits and takes money out of many pockets.* HE *takes out a huge money roll, already bound with a large rubber band.*)

CHARLEY
(*Gaping at it.*) Wow! It has so many layers. It's like an onion!

JOSE
(*The elastic shoots into the air.*) Get that, Charley! I don't want to lose that. These elastics, strong like that, are hard to get. This roll is big enough, I'm not going to put any more in it. I'm going to start a new one. (**HE** *reaches in his pockets and takes out more bills.* **HE** *spreads the money on the floor between them.*) Look at all this money, Charley. Did you ever see so much money? I bet you never have.

CHARLEY
No, I never have, Pa.

111

JOSE
(*Sadly.*) But I can't keep it all. I have to spend some. I have to buy food for you, Charley. I have to fill up your belly.

ILDA
(*Enters kitchen looking for* **CHARLEY**. **SHE** *calls up to the attic.*) Jose! (*Pause.*) Are you up there?

JOSE
Yes!

ILDA
Is Charley with you?

JOSE
Yes!

ILDA
What are you doing?

JOSE
Nothing! Go about your business, woman!

ILDA
It's too cold up there! You're both going to get sick!

JOSE
It's warm up here!

ILDA
Liar!

JOSE
(*To* **CHARLEY**.) Even up here, you can't get away from her. She seeks you out. She has to stick her nose in everywhere.

ILDA
I'm married to a crazy man!

JOSE
(**THEY** *resume counting and looking at the money.*) Look at this, Charley! A twenty! You don't see many of these. Think of how many shoes I had to fix to get this. This came from a Frenchman. He tried to play a trick on me. He gave me this for a small job, a twenty-five-cent job. He was hoping I couldn't make change. Then he'd get the work done free. But I fooled him. I had the money. I said to him, 'I'm not the bank. Don't you got something smaller?' 'No,' he said, 'that's all I got.' The son of a whore. But I know all their tricks.

ILDA
Jose! Send that child down here right now! It's too cold for him up there! He's going to get sick!

JOSE
He'll be down in a minute.

ILDA
I know what your minutes are like! Charley, come down here right now!

JOSE
(**CHARLEY** *stands. In a low voice.*) Stay. Let her wait.

ILDA
You're going to be responsible for whatever happens, not me! (**SHE** *mutters something under breath.*)

JOSE
Let her scream. It'll do her good. It clears the blood. But what a powerful voice she has. For certainty she could raise the dead. This is a good job we did, Charley. A very good piece of work. (**HE** *stands.*) But it all goes out. It doesn't all stay, Charley. Never think that. Twenty dollars to your mother for the house. Tomorrow I have to give the Jew six dollars for rent. I have to buy supplies. One way or another, it goes. (*Lights dim on attic.* **CHARLEY** *exits to kitchen where* **ILDA** *is waiting.* **JOSE** *walks to shop.*)

Lights up on shop, and on **CHARLES,** *who is watching.*

CHARLES
Money was life. Money was food and shelter. Money was coal in the cellar. So he loved money because he loved life. Someone once said, 'Every man's life has a book in it.' If so, my father's book was his bankbook. He came to an agreement with the Creator of the Universe (*To* **JOSE,** *as* **THE CREATOR.**) 'Let's make a deal, Joe. You give me a lifetime of unceasing toil and I will give you a little book with some numbers in it. It's called a bankbook.'

JOSE
That sounds like a good deal. I'll take it!

CHARLES
Would it have been any different in Portugal? In Portugal there was no money, so there was no need to get excited. But America! He was amazed to discover he could make money here and he never got over it. It set his mouth to watering. He was like a kid picking blueberries in a patch of woods on Shawmut Avenue.

Lights come up on radio station. **JOSE** *sits in shop and listens to the radio.*

113

Radio Ensemble
(*Enter to microphone.*)

Trudi
(*Singing.*) w-n-b-h… New Bedford…

Shannon
…broadcasting from the New Bedford Hotel…

Ben

This, today! A cobbler shop in the South End of New Bedford was blown up yesterday. The owner of the shop believes it is the work of the organized labor movement, as union leaders are pressuring cobblers and shoemakers in New Bedford to organize and form a union of their own…

Jose *is listening to the radio.* **He** *turns it off, and runs home.* **Ilda** *and* **Charley** *are in the kitchen.*

Ilda
(*To* **Jose** *as he enters kitchen.*) What are you doing home so early?

Jose
(*Agitated. Running throughout the kitchen.*) They blew up a cobbler shop in the South End! Tommy, the Fish and Chips Man, brought me the paper. I'm next! I'm next! Quick! Get me something to eat! I have to get back to the shop before it gets dark. I have to stay there tonight and guard it. It's the only thing I can do.

Ilda
I don't want you going back there tonight, Jose! It's too dangerous!

Jose
I know that fellow Lemieux has a gun. I'm going to his house to borrow it.

Ilda
(*Overlapping with* **Jose**.) A gun! Are you crazy? You don't know any-

thing about guns! You'll kill yourself!

JOSE
This is how they unionize. With bombs. They're gangsters. Filth. So this is what America has come to!

ILDA
I don't want you to go, Jose! Let them blow it up! What do you care? It's not your building! All you've got in there is some junky old machines! It's not worth losing your life over!

115

JOSE
Woman, you're giving me a headache! Just give me my food! Let this matter with me! Charley, you'll come with me. (**CHARLEY** *stands.*)

ILDA
No, he stays! Don't you have any shame at all, man? You would place your own son in danger for the sake of that filthy hole you call a shop? He stays! You go if you want to! Get yourself blown up! But he stays!

JOSE *makes the journey back to the shop.* **CHARLEY** *and* **ILDA** *watch from the window.*
I'm not going to be able to sleep a wink tonight. That crazy man. He causes me so much worry.

JOSE
(*At bench in shop, holding weapon.*) The Union wants to tell me how much to charge and how long to work. My own business, they would run it for me. I will close my door first, before I let them tell me one thing to do. This is all the work of that son of a whore Roosevelt. He has encouraged these gangsters. I should have voted for Hoover. I make a big mistake there. (**JOSE** *sits, guarding shop. Long dim of lights as projections of* **CHARLIE CHAPLIN** *appear on stage behind* **JOSE**.)

ILDA
(*Standing at window. Speaking to* **CHARLEY** *at first.*) He wasn't always the way he is now. He wasn't so serious. He liked to have some fun. When

we were first married, he used to take me to the movies. On Sunday he would dress up in his suit and take me to the Olympia downtown. He was crazy for Charlie Chaplin. No picture of Charlie Chaplin came but he didn't take me by the hand and rush me downtown to see it. 'I don't want to miss this,' he'd say. Funny pictures he liked. The dramas he didn't like so well because he couldn't follow the words too good. I'd have to be explaining to him what happened. But even then he was trying to save money. We never sat in the expensive seats at the Olympia. They were downstairs. He always took me upstairs to the second balcony, where the screen was a thousand miles away. Nigger heaven, they used to call it.

Once, when we were first married, I went to his shop and it was closed! He was in the barroom two doors down, drinking with his cronies. He was drinking that muscatel wine that he so likes. I had to go in there and drag him out by the ear. More than once that happened, too. But, no more. (**Charley** *exits to kitchen table.*)

I told him, 'Let's go. Let's go visit Portugal, see your Father!' With his money, he could live like a king over there. He refuses. He doesn't want to go. He's afraid everything will be different, and he won't know anything. I would like to go. I'm sure not everything would be changed. There would be much there the same as when I was a young girl. (*Thinking about Portugal.*) When I was a little girl in Portugal, I loved the hot chestnuts. The man used to come around in his little wagon. He'd cry out, *'Castanhas! Castanhas!'* and all the kids would come running. It was just like when the ice-cream man comes around in this country. He'd roast them right in front of us. They were one cent each. Oh, they tasted so good!

(**Sound:** *Fado Music, images of* **Portugal** *appear on stage. Eventually,* **Ilda** *enters kitchen.* **Jose** *and* **Charley** *are sitting at table.* **Daughter,** **Idalia,** *is helping* **Ilda.**)

Ilda
(*Handing* **Jose** *a pickle jar.*) Here, man. Open this.

Jose
(**He** *strains to twist the top.*) Try it now.

ILDA

(*Teasing him.*) Oh, what a big strong man I have here. Oh, so proud he is! Nobody else is so able. Nobody else is so talented.

JOSE

I close up the shop Thursday morning and I went to the bank in the South End.

IDALIA

Oh, did you take some money out? (**ALL** *laugh.*)

117

JOSE

I was chagrined! I forgot where it was. It's been so long since I was there. I got off the streetcar many blocks too soon. I had to walk a long way. I felt like a fool.

ILDA

Why didn't you look out the window before you got off.

JOSE

There is no time for that. There is no time for looking. The streetcar only stops a second. You have to get out quick if you're going to get out.

IDALIA

Why didn't you ask the conductor to let you know when he came to the bank?

JOSE

What? And have everybody know where I was going? Are you crazy? I don't want nobody to know I'm going to a bank!

ILDA

He thinks everybody has it in their mind to rob him.

IDALIA

Pa, why do you go all the way to the South End for a bank? Why don't you put your money in the bank on Davis Street? It's so close to us, you could just walk there.

JOSE
No. That's no good. You never want to go to a bank near where you live. There people know you and when they see you walking in the bank, they start talking among themselves. 'I think that fellow's got money.' Pretty soon comes a knock on the door. They want a loan. In the South End it doesn't matter who sees me. Nobody knows me there. I'm safe.

ILDA
He even goes out of town to a bank. He has money in a bank in Fairhaven. To get there he has to take a streetcar downtown and then he has to change. He has to get on a Fairhaven streetcar and cross the Fairhaven Bridge. Next he'll be going to a bank on Cape Cod so that when he wants to put some money in the bank, he can spend the whole day traveling there and back.

JOSE
I don't want nobody to know my business.

IDALIA
Why don't you just pick one bank and keep all your money there?

JOSE
No. That's no good. Then what happens if that bank fails? Then you're out of luck. It's better to have your money in more than one bank. Then you have better protection. If one bank fails, maybe the other won't.

ILDA
Don't you know that Roosevelt has changed the law? Now the banks cannot fail. Your money is safe there now. It's guaranteed by the government.

JOSE
Donkey shit for Roosevelt! Do you think I would believe anything that

rascal says? Roosevelt says one thing today and a different thing tomorrow. I don't trust him.

ILDA

I know you have money at the Five Cents Savings downtown on Purchase Street. That would be a good place because it's centrally located. You could keep all your money there. You wouldn't have to be going such great distances to put some money in.

JOSE

What do you care where I keep my money? I'm going to look at that bankbook. I haven't had a chance to look at it yet.

119

ILDA

That precious bank book of yours! You should have it memorized by now. Do you think your staring at it is going to make it grow?

JOSE

Yes. It is growing while I am looking at it. They pay me interest.

ILDA

When they see you, they say, 'Here is a cheapskate with a suit a hundred years' old.'

JOSE

What the hell do I care what they say? Do they put food on my table? Huh? No. So what the hell do I care what they say? This is the only thing that America understands—money! (**HE** *waves his bankbook in the air.*) Then they respect you. They tip their hat to you and say, 'Good morning, Mr. Felix. How are you today?'

ILDA

It hurts him to spend. He doesn't want to spend on nothing. That's his way. He'll never change now. We got electricity years after everybody else got it. He didn't want to pay the expense of the electrician. We were the last house on the street to get it. Maybe the last house in New Bedford.

JOSE
I don't make you wipe your ass with newspaper like Fragoza does his wife.

ILDA
That's different. Fragoza has no money! You do! You know, in Portugal they tell this fable. A beggar found a big roll of bills. That night he put it under his pillow but he could not sleep. He lay awake waiting for somebody to come rob him. After three nights like that, the beggar seized the money and threw it out of the window. 'All it brought me was lack of sleep,' he said. 'Now I can sleep easy.' Are you listening to me, Mister Moneybags? Do you understand the lesson of the story?

JOSE
You come at me with a fable? You want me to base my life on a fairy tale?

ILDA
It's supposed to make you think!

JOSE
Take your damn fable to the store and try to buy a loaf of bread with it!
(*Lights down on kitchen, and up on shop, as* **JOSE** *and* **CHARLEY** *walk to shop.*)

RADIO ENSEMBLE
(*Enter to microphone. Singing.*)
New Bedford Institution for Savings
Makes banking easy as can be.
With four handy branches in your neighborhood
Bank conveniently.
So, let your money make money for you
And give you personal service, too.
New Bedford Institution for Savings
Makes more money for you!

BEN
From Europe: The Germans have invaded the Soviet Union!

RADIO ENSEMBLE
(*Singing.*) W-N-B-H. New Bedford. (**THEY** *exit.*)
Lights down on **ENSEMBLE** *and up on* **JOSE** *and* **CHARLEY** *in the cobbler shop.*

JOSE
(**JOSE** *in the shop with* **CHARLEY**. **THEY** *are working. After a while.*)
Guess how much I'm worth today, Charley. Not counting the houses. Just cash money. Cash in the bank.

121

CHARLEY
I don't know, Pa.

JOSE
I know you don't know. That's why I'm asking you to guess.

CHARLEY
I wouldn't have any idea, Pa.

JOSE
I know that. But I want you to guess anyway. Take a guess. Go ahead. Take a guess. How much do you think I am worth?

CHARLEY
(*To* **JOSE**, *blurting it out.*) Ten thousand dollars.

JOSE
No! More than that! Take another guess!

CHARLEY
Fifteen thousand dollars.

JOSE
No! More than that yet!

CHARLEY
I don't know, Pa. How much?

JOSE
Twenty thousand dollars! More than twenty! Over twenty! (HE *laughs, radiant.*) Not bad for a dumb foreigner, huh?

CHARLEY
No, that's good, Pa. Very good.

JOSE
I came to this country with just the shirt on my back. I couldn't speak a word of English. People look at you like you're a piece of shit. But how many of those who lived here and could speak English—how many of those have twenty thousand dollars today, I'd like to know! Hah!

CHARLEY
There's not many who have done as good as you have, Pa.

JOSE
People pass by and they see this tiny little shop, everything very modest, they think, 'Ah, what a poor shop. He must not make enough to live on in there.' They would never guess how much I made here. Nobody even suspects. Your mother makes fun of this place. She calls it a dirty little hole. Well, maybe it is, but this is where I made my money. But I had to work very hard for it, Charley. It wasn't growing on the trees. Never think it was easy. Never think that for even one minute! How many thousands of nails did I have to bang in! Sometimes, on Saturday night, I was so tired I could hardly see the nails. I did it all with my two arms. I have money in three banks, just imagine! Twenty thousand dollars! I came to this country without a pot to piss in. And today I am worth more than twenty thousand dollars! Who would believe such a thing is possible? (HE *gazes into the distance. Pause.*) I'm not rich but I'm certainly not poor either. What would they call me? Middle class?

CHARLEY
Yes, I guess so, Pa.

JOSE
(*Crosses downstage, alone.*) America is a fine place, but if you don't have money in America, watch out! They let you die like a dog in the corner! They let you turn your face to the wall and die like a dog. If you don't have money in this country, they give you a kick to the gutter like a dog. You need money in America. Without money, nobody cares for you. (*Long fade on* JOSE. HE *exits.*)

RADIO ENSEMBLE
(*At microphone. Singing.* CHARLEY *is listening to the radio as* HE *sweeps up the shop.*)
Things go better with Coca-Cola,
Things go better with Coke.

123

SHANNON
With its life and sparkle, Coca-Cola is a natural part of social occasions. You feel at ease drinking something that makes a pause... the "pause that refreshes." Coca-Cola, America's favorite moment.

BEN
Coca-Cola is visiting New Bedford! ...you must be home to win! It's like money falling out of the sky, folks! The Coca-Cola guys are even now loading up a carrying case with Coca-Cola bottles. In seconds they will be on your corner, in your neighborhood!
(**RADIO ENSEMBLE** *exit.* CHARLEY *finishes sweeping shop and runs home.*)

CHARLEY
(*Standing in the doorway, looking out.*) Ma! There's a guy coming to the house! He's giving away free Cokes!

ILDA
What do I want with your *merda* of Cokes?

CHARLEY
They're free, Ma!

ILDA

I know their tricks! Sure, here, take it, it's free. Then afterwards, pay!

CHARLEY

No, Ma. He's not going to charge you. He just wants you to try it out. He's coming to every house. It's a free sample.

ILDA

I don't want no Cokes.

CHARLEY

But it's free!

ILDA

I don't want none, free or no free. When I want some, I'll buy it. I know where the store is. Those people don't give away something for nothing. I don't want none.

CHARLEY

Well, if you don't want one, at least let me have one.

ILDA

No. You want one? Save your money and buy it.

CHARLEY

(*Desperately.*) Ma, I've never had a Coke!

ILDA

Well, it hasn't killed you so far.

CHARLEY

Ma, I want to see what it tastes like.

ILDA

No.

CHARLEY
But it's free! It won't cost you anything! Let me have one, Ma.

ILDA
No. Why should I take it? I know that I'm not going to buy any. It would just be fooling him. I have no money for Cokes. (*Stands at door, and shakes* **HER** *head to* **COCA-COLA MAN.**)

CHARLEY
What if Butch asks me if I've ever had one? I don't even know what it tastes like! What if someone at New Bedford High school asks me? (**ILDA** *exits.*) What if a West End girl does? I don't dream about the North End girls anymore. I like the West End girls. They have class. They are beautiful, carefree girls with tennis racquets on their shoulders, and they gather at the net for the *Pause that Refreshes.*

(**MUSIC—ALL THE THINGS ARE YOU.** *Images of Coca-Cola ads appear.* **CHARLEY** *walks toward the images and stands with them.* **HE** *tries a few swings of an imaginary tennis racket, as music fades and images dim.*)

CHARLES
(*Lights up on classroom, stage right.*) 'Oh, North is North, and West is West, and never the twain shall meet.' The West End girls now occupied my dream life. And I constructed my dreams the way Communists write history. I deleted, altered, fabricated. I excised dark moments of reality. In September I got on a streetcar and went downtown to the centrally located New Bedford High School. It was like going out into America for the first time. It seemed that almost all the kids from the North End picked the Commercial course. But almost all the kids from the West End picked the College course. They were now my classmates. They were Yankees. They lived in the nice part of town. They did not live in tenements. The mothers spoke excellent English. The fathers wore white shirts and ties to work. The daughters did not work in sweatshops. These were people with lawns and telephones and automobiles. These were people with running hot water. These were people without any taint of foreignness. These were the real Americans.

Lights down…

END of **ACT I**

ACT TWO

Lights come up on the Felix family kitchen in the North End of New Bedford, Massachusetts. JOSE *is sitting at the table.* ILDA *is serving.*

JOSE
(*Thinking.*) Audette the Paint Man came to see me today. He offered me the house of the Communist for twenty-two hundred dollars. It's a good price. A very good price.

ILDA
What did you tell him?

JOSE
I told him no. I said, 'Audette, I don't need no more houses. I don't want no more houses. I got two houses now. That's enough. I got enough headaches now,' I told him. 'I don't need no more headaches.'

ILDA
For once you did the right thing. You're working yourself to death now. You don't need another responsibility.

JOSE
(*Laughs*) Audette came to me because he knows it would be an easy sale, no bother. There are not many buyers around who can put two thousand dollars down on the table within minutes. I never told him, but somehow that rascal knows I got money. The house is in good repair. It doesn't need nothing. Not like the drunkard's house. (*Pause.*) The Communist is a good tenant. She is a lady of quiet habits. She doesn't drink, so she does not damage the house. And she always pays the rent on time. Somehow she always works.

(*Lights flicker to show passage of time.*)

JOSE
It's a nice house.

ILDA
What house?

JOSE
The Communist's house.

ILDA
You're still talking about that house? I thought you told Audette no.

JOSE
I did.

ILDA
Then what are you talking about it for?

JOSE
(*Shrugs.*) It doesn't do any harm to talk about it.

ILDA
Are you changing your mind about it?

JOSE
No, I'm not changing my mind. I'm not going to buy it. (*Pause.*) This is good soup. What do I need another house for? No. I'm not buying the house.

(*Lights flicker to show passage of time.*)

JOSE
(*At front door.*) I didn't sleep at all last night, thinking about that damn house. The whole night I was awake.

ILDA
Just make up your mind, man! Either buy it or don't buy it! But make up your mind one way or the other. Come to some decision. Otherwise it's going to make you sick.

JOSE
I've made up my mind. I'm not going to buy it. I'll tell Audette tomorrow. (*A beat.*)

I don't want the house. I've got no use for the house.
(*Lights flicker to show passage of time.*)

JOSE
I bought the house. It's a nice house. I'll have to deal with the
Communist, though, but I already know her. She is my customer. (**HE**
walks to shop.)

MRS. D'HAZE
(**MRS. MAUD D'HAZE** *enters through auditorium, handing out
Communist propaganda pamphlets to everyone.*) To each according to his   *131*
need! From each according to his ability! Everyone will contribute.

JOSE
(*Calling to* **MRS. D'HAZE**.) Hey! These bums here in Weld Square.
What are they going to con-tribute?

MRS. D'HAZE
(*Calling back.*) These bums have been demoralized by the capitalist system! There are no bums in the Soviet Union! No bums. No prostitutes.
No hunger. No bread lines. No unemployment. No misery. No jails,
because wrongdoers are reeducated and returned to society as produc-
tive citizens. All in all, who wouldn't want to live in the Soviet Union?
Where did it all go wrong? (**SHE** *climbs stairs to stage.*)

JOSE
(*To audience.*) That woman is so dense, it hurts my head to talk to her.
When I see her coming, I turn on my machines, so I won't have to hear
her. There are some people who believe angels are flying around in the
sky. She is a person like that. (*To* **MRS. D'HAZE**.) The trouble is, once
you got that system, you say something, they shoot you. (**HE** *and*
CHARLEY *enter shop.*)

MRS. D'HAZE
(**SHE** *enters shop.*) I've come to pay the rent. Three dollars a week.

JOSE
Good.

MRS. D'HAZE
You know, nobody pays rent in the Soviet Union

JOSE
(*Nods understandingly.*) Everything is free there. The workers own the housing. It's a wonderful place. I'm surprised you don't go there.

MRS. D'HAZE
Rent is capitalistic exploitation of the workers. It doesn't exist in the Soviet Union.

(**JOSE** *nods as she pokes about her purse and takes out crumpled bills.*)

JOSE
Thank you. Put the money in the box, Charley. (**HE** *hands the money to* **CHARLEY.**)

MRS. D'HAZE
(**MRS. D'HAZE** *stands there, waiting.*) Where's my receipt?

JOSE
(**HE** *stares at her a moment, dumfounded.*) What do you need a receipt for?

MRS. D'HAZE
I want proof I paid you.

JOSE
What do you take me for, a crook? You think I'm going to crook you?

MRS. D'HAZE
It's just good business practice, Joe. It's my right to have one and I want it.

JOSE

I got two other houses. I don't give nobody receipts.

MRS. D'HAZE

It's for my records.

JOSE

Next thing you're going to ask for a receipt when I fix your shoes.

MRS. D'HAZE

I don't have any proof I paid you.

133

JOSE

Proof? Proof? You think I'm going to go to you and ask for the rent twice?

MRS. D'HAZE

I'm entitled to a receipt.

JOSE

When you give me the money, I know you paid me.

MRS. D'HAZE

That's beside the point. I want proof.

JOSE

You don't trust me.

MRS. D'HAZE

The whole capitalist system is rotten to its very foundation. Why should I trust you?

JOSE

Yes, you're always talking about heaven, but you don't trust nobody.

MRS. D'HAZE

That's different, Joe! That's the Soviet Union! That's not here! In the

Soviet Union you can trust your fellow man! Everything belongs to the people! The profits go to the common good! The workers own the factories! There are no bosses there to live off your sweat. Wake up, Joe! There's no J.P. Morgan in the Soviet Union!

JOSE
(*Glaring at* **HER.**) I will give you a receipt... (**HE** *rips apart an empty heel box and hands* **CHARLEY** *a piece of it.*) Write on there, Charley, that she gave me three dollars.

MRS. D'HAZE
You don't have a receipt book? You can get them from Woolworth's for ten cents.

JOSE
I don't have one. This is all I got.

MRS. D'HAZE
It's not a proper receipt.

JOSE
Sign it, Charley.

MRS. D'HAZE
You have to sign it.

JOSE
I don't sign my name for nobody!

MRS. D'HAZE
He's underage. His signature has no legal standing in court.

JOSE
Court? Court? You're taking me to court now? I knew I shouldn't have bought that damn house!

Mrs. D'Haze
Don't get so excited. I'm not taking you to court.

Jose
Well, I don't sign it. You think I got nothing better to do than spend my day signing papers? (**He** *turns to* **Charley**, *enraged.*) That woman is a pestilence. Yes, she's a pestilence. I'm going to kick her out!
(*Lights flicker to show passage of time.* **Jose** *and* **Mrs. D'Haze** *freeze facing away from each other.*)

Jose   *135*
(*Turning back to* **Mrs. D'Haze**.) I am well content with you. Yes, well content. There's no use you making the trip every Saturday here. I'm going to save you the trouble. I'm going to send my boy over to your house every Saturday afternoon. You pay him and he will give you the receipt. That way you can stay home and rest yourself. (**She** *exits. To* **Charley**.) I don't want her coming to the shop. Her tongue is never still. She doesn't even stop to take a breath. I don't want to hear any more shit about Russia. (**Charley** *exits to collect rent.*)

Charley
(**Charley** *at door.*) I'm here for the rent.

Mrs. D'Haze
(*Entering.*) I was on the throne, boy! Do you know what that means? (**She** *laughs.*)
You want to know the truth, boy? Here, read this! (*Waves a pamphlet in the air.*) This will give you the truth! And the truth shall make you free! Don't believe the newspapers! It's all lies! Lies! Lies! Learn the truth, boy! There are no bread lines in the Soviet Union! Do you know that, boy? And you know why? Because they have a Five-Year Plan!

Charles
(*Enters with sign that says "Russian War Relief."*) No bread lines. Only, in Shostakovich's phrase, mountains of corpses. What if the "plan" is to kill all the Jews? (*Hands sign to* **Mrs. D'Haze**.)

Radio Ensemble
(*Enter to microphone.*)

Shannon
Reporting today. From the continent… The Russians have stopped the German advance.

Ben
In the North, the German attack advanced only ten kilometers into the Russian lines in two days, and was stopped after losing twenty-thousand soldiers and two hundred tanks. After a week of heavy fighting with heavy casualties on both sides, the temperature at thirteen degrees below zero, the Germans, benumbed with cold and debilitated by the fatigue of their long effort, were in poor condition to meet the Russian's thundering blows. Initially, they buckled from the pressure, and then recovered. The Red Army, sensing victory, hit them again. This time the Germans collapsed and retreated.

Trudi
Remember to tune in to wnbh for all of the latest news from the Front.

(**Ensemble** *exit.*)

Mrs. D'Haze
(*Speaking and waving the sign as* **She** *exits through auditorium.*) No one believed me! I told everybody this was going to happen but they didn't believe me! The Russian workers are fighting bravely. Do you know why? Because they own the means of production! They're not fighting for capitalists! They're fighting for themselves! (**She** *continues as she exits through auditorium.*)

Charles
I think of Mrs. D'Haze fondly. She was a believer in fairy tales. She hungered for a new world, a world of fairness and caring. Scorned by all, laughed at openly, her message unheeded, she never wavered. In some ways she reminds me of myself. She spent her free time in fruitless harangues to uncaring listeners. I spend my free time writing and send-

ing manuscripts to uncaring editors. My words fall on deaf ears, just as hers did. But she never gave up. And I haven't either. We're just a couple of nuts. (**CHARLES** *sits at desk in his classroom and types.*)
Lights ups on the cobbler shop. **JOSE** *&* **CHARLEY** *have been working for some time. It is very hot. We hear the hammering of nails into the shoes.* **CHARLES** *watches from classroom.*

JOSE
(*After a while.*) Do you want to take rest, Charley?

CHARLEY   *137*
No.

JOSE
Take this one outside with the screwdriver. (**CHARLEY** *runs outside with shoe.* **JOSE** *calls out to him.*) That's the shoe of the Polocka gravedigger. That's what all the mud is from. He's a gravedigger. What a great shoe that Polocka has. I could fit two of mine in the one. (*Pause.*) Well, it's steady work. There's always someone who dies.

(**CHARLEY** *returns with the shoe. They work for a while in silence.*) So you want to go to college, Charley?

CHARLEY
Yes, I would like to go, Pa.

JOSE
(*Looking deep into his son's eyes.*) All right, then. I will send you.

CHARLEY
Thank you, Pa.

JOSE
If I can give you a push up, I will be glad to do it.

CHARLES / **CHARLEY**
(*To audience, repeating.*) 'If I can give you a push up, I will be glad to do it.'

JOSE
This cobbler business is no good for you, Charley. You have to work too hard, too many hours, to make any money. It's all right for me, that's my life, I'm not complaining. But maybe you can pick up something better.

CHARLES
'If I can give you a push up, I will be glad to do it.'

CHARLEY
138 Thank you, Pa!

JOSE
(**THEY** *finish the shoes.*) There's a good job! A very good job. Take fifteen cents out of the cashbox, Charley, and go to the store across the street and get us a big bottle of soda.

CHARLEY
What kind should I get, Pa?

JOSE
Whatever kind you want. As long as it's cold.

(**CHARLEY** *runs off and returns with the bottle of soda.* **THEY** *share it.*)

JOSE
Aahh. It's good, Charley. Drink up. What kind was that?

CHARLEY
It's Coca Cola, Pa. It's something like sarsparilla.

JOSE
(*Resting for a moment. Then, with a start.*) Go get the five cents back before they forget you bought it there! Go there tomorrow and they won't give you your money back. They'll say you didn't buy it there! Go today!

(**Charley** *runs off to redeem bottle. Music*—**Roll Out The Barrel**
Lights down on shop.)
Lights up on the piazza of the family home. **Charley** *runs home and sits*
on the piazza with Idalia. **They** *are reading a newspaper.* **Music** *'Ain't*
Misbehavin' *under scene.*

Idalia
This is Pa reading the *Diario de Noticias! (Moving her lips as* **She** *reads.*
They *laugh.*)

Charley   *139*
(*Taking newspaper from* **Idalia**.) No, no! This is it! (*Imitating his father,*
He *reads silently, moving his lips and muttering.*) 'Donkey shit!'… 'Son of
a whore! He attached the dog. Yes he did!'

Ilda
(*Enters piazza, catching them.* **She** *has a sleeve of Ritz crackers in her*
hand.) What are you doing? You shouldn't do that! (*In Portuguese.*) You
should be ashamed! Your father was poor when he lived in Portugal. He
could not go to school. He had to go to work. If he had gone to school
like you, then he would be able to read like you. But you should never
make fun of him. It's not his fault. (*Exits to kitchen.*)

Idalia
(**Charley** *and* **Idalia** *exchange looks.* **Idalia** *to* **Charley**.) What a jerk
you are!
(*Hands him the college catalogues.*) Pick out the college you want,
Charley. What do you want to be, Charley?

Charley
I don't know. (**Ilda** *returns to the piazza and sits with them.*)

Idalia
How about being a doctor?

Charley
Hmmmmm.

IDALIA
Yes, you could be a doctor. But when you take that knife and operate on a person, all that blood comes running out. I wouldn't like that.

ILDA
A doctor can do much good. He alleviates suffering.

IDALIA
But when somebody dies, they can blame you for it. Why don't you be a lawyer, Charley? You like to talk.

ILDA
There are too many lawyers already. They sit downtown in their offices killing flies.

IDALIA
Well, I know one lawyer who has all the business he wants. Secundo B. Alves. Did you see what he did at the parade of the *Festa da Madeira?* He grabbed the Portuguese flag and ran with it to the head of the parade, ahead of the American flag. (**THEY** *laugh together.*) He started a big fight!

CHARLEY
Senhor Fragoza said, 'I'd rather be held up by a man with a gun than have a lawyer come at him waving a piece of paper. I'd lose less money.'

IDALIA
What about being a dentist? (**THEY** *continue looking at catalogues and listening to the radio.* **THEY** *hear a radio report about "jobs of the future."*)

RADIO ENSEMBLE
(*Enter to microphone.*)

TRUDI
Hey everybody! We want to remind you to buy up those war bonds and support our boys (*Singing.*) 'Over there.' And, now, "God Bless America," by Irving Berlin:

'While the storm clouds gather far across the sea,
Let us swear allegiance to a land that's free
Let us all be grateful for a land so fair
As we raise our voices in a solemn prayer.
God Bless America
Land that I love
Stand beside her,
And guide her
Through the night
With the light from above.'

141

BEN
That was the lovely voice of Miss Miller.
The Standard Times is reporting on jobs of the future, and it seems that they predict a shortage of Pharmacists. There are just a handful of schools that offer a degree in pharmacy, and these schools are turning out just a few graduates. You see, the State has passed a law. You have to have a registered pharmacist in the store at all times, so that's why so many are needed. They expect a big shortage of pharmacists in the years ahead. If you are graduating from New Bedford High School this year, why not head to pharmacy school?
(*Singing with* IDALIA *from piazza.*) W-N-B-H

IDALIA/CHARLEY
Pharmacist!

CHARLEY
(HE *runs to shop where* JOE *is working.*) Pa! I was reading this article in the Standard Times on jobs of the future. They expect a big shortage of pharmacists. See, the reason is that there are just a handful of schools that offer a degree in pharmacy, and these schools are turning out just a few graduates. What do you think about my being a pharmacist?

JOSE
Pharmacist would be good, Charley! It's just like shoemaker, except higher class!
(*Lights down on shop.*)

Lights up on front of stage, in **Cabral's** *pharmacy.*

Charles
(*Speaking as he is dressing up as* **Pharmacist Cabral**—*Lab coat, monocle, wig, mustache.*) Say the word "operation" or "hospital" to a Portuguese in New Bedford in the 1930s, and he would turn pale. He didn't really hear those words. His brain had jumped ahead to the next word, "cemetery." The Portuguese had a paralyzing fear of the hospital. They believed that the hospital had a one-way door. People went there to die, if not immediately, a few days later. And this was often true, because the Portuguese patient waited to enter the hospital until he was past help. So, for the Portuguese, the hospital was out as part of their medical delivery system. They limited themselves to the ministrations of Cabral the Pharmacist. (*As* **Cabral.** *Slapstick-like to the gathering crowd of* **Ladies.**) As advertised this tonic cures weakness in the legs and sourness in the stomach. It will make you feel younger, restore iron to the blood, invigorate the liver, cleanse the whole system of its poisons, and do about eight other things.

Lady #1
(*Speaking with a group of* **Ladies** *that has gathered on the street in front of the pharmacy.*) I don't feel good. I think I'm going to go see Cabral.

Lady #2
Oh, yes! He does much good. He knows as much as any doctor, maybe more.

Lady #3
And he didn't learn from any books. He learned from experience. He is a man of great experience.

Lady #1
In my land they say a donkey in a white suit is called a doctor!

Ladies
(*All agree, saying this in Portuguese.*)

CABRAL
(*Placing a chair for* **LADY #1** *with a flourish. He exhibits a wonderful "sofa-side" manner.*) Dear lady. How can I possibly help you?

LADY #1
Oh, Senhor Cabral, I don't know where to turn! I have terrible pain in my back. Sometimes it hurts so much it brings tears to my eyes.

CABRAL
Ooohh, dear lady, how you must have suffered! Here, try this!

143

LADY #1
Oh, Senhor Cabral. I'm sure this will help. I know you understand.

CABRAL
(*To audience.*) You see? She's starting to feel better already. (**HE** *pats her on the rump, and she exits.* **LADY #2** *sits down.*)

LADY #2
Senhor, please help me. I cannot sleep at night.

CABRAL
(*Eyeing her lasciviously. Winking to audience.*) Such misery! Is there pain?

LADY #2
Yes, oh yes. It shoots up and down my back.

CABRAL
(*Massaging her backside.*) Terrible, terrible, terrible.

LADY #2
What have I done to be plagued this way?

CABRAL
You have endured much. Is it worse in the morning, or at night?

LADY #2

Sometimes at night, sometimes in the morning.

CABRAL

Ah! (**HE** *holds up a bottle of a rich-green liquid to the light and moves it this way and that.*) This medicine has helped many with your condition. I have every confidence it will help you. (*To* **LADY #3**, *who has entered.*) This is not one medicine, but five medicines in this bottle. If one ingredient does not help you, another one will. But (**HE** *pauses for effect*) I must warn you. It is not cheap. I could give you a cheaper medicine. It has only two ingredients. But I cannot recommend it with the confidence as I can this one.

LADY #3

No, no. I want this one!

CABRAL

That is a wise choice, dear lady. When it comes to matters of health, one should not be looking for bargains.

LADY #1

Money! Money! Who cares about money with the pain I have?

CABRAL

Exactly so! It is better to be without money and have your health than it is to be with money and not have your health. Is that not so?

LADY #2

Will it taste bad?

CABRAL

No. On the contrary, dear lady, it will taste so good you will be tempted to take more than the dosage I am going to prescribe for you. But you must not do that. This medicine contains a drug—not opium, but with an action similar to opium. It puts the body to sleep. And while the nerves are asleep, another ingredient in the medicine attacks and destroys the source of the inflammation that is causing this pain. They are soldiers who will isolate the enemy camp and overpower it, conquer it, and end this turmoil within your body.

LADIES
Oh, bless you. Bless you, Senhor Cabral, bless you.
(*We hear* **SIREN** *and Police whistle in the distance. Keystone Cops style* **MUSIC***.*)

CABRAL
(**HE** *packs up things in a hurry.*) Don't count on anything! (**CABRAL** *exits.* **LADIES** *exit.*
Lights, Sound out.)

145

Lights up in kitchen.

ILDA
(**ILDA** *hears the mailman deliver a letter.*) That's the mailman! Go down and get the mail, huh, Charley? (**CHARLEY** *runs to the mailbox and returns with a letter.*)

Ooohh, what is this now? What calamity is this? (**ILDA** *reads the letter. Some spoken in Portuguese. After a pause.*) It's the father of your father. He has died. This is going to hit your father very hard. He was a poor cobbler in Portugal, your Vivou. Your father loved him very much even though they were far away from each other.

CHARLEY
The picture in your bedroom?

ILDA
Yes.

JOSE
(**JOSE** *enters kitchen, laughing as he enters.*) That rascal Cabral! He's in trouble again. They're gonna shut down his operation! (**HE** *sits at the table, laughing.*)

ILDA
A letter came for you today, Jose. (**SHE** *shows him the letter and reads it to him.* **HE** *slumps in his chair.* **SHE** *comforts him.* **MUSIC—** **SHOSTAKOVITCH.** **ILDA** *exits.* **JOSE** *sits alone and listens to music. Lights fade.*)

CHARLEY
(*Time passes. Lights up.* **CHARLEY** *enters kitchen. To* **JOSE**.) I'm going to the University of Michigan, Pa.

146

JOSE
To be pharmacist, Charley? (*Frowning.*) That's in the state of Michigan? (**ILDA** *enters.*)

CHARLEY
Yes.

JOSE
That's on the other side of Pennsylvania, isn't it?

CHARLEY
Yes, it is.

JOSE
Why so far away, Charley?

ILDA
(*Sadly.*) I don't like you being so far away. Something could happen.

CHARLEY
What could happen?

ILDA
You could get sick.

CHARLEY
I'm not going to get sick, Ma.

ILDA
How do you know? Nobody knows when they're going to get sick.

CHARLEY
Well, I'm sure they have plenty of doctors and a hospital there. There's so many students. They have to provide for them.

ILDA
I don't like it.

CHARLEY
The trouble with you is you think I'm a little baby. I'm old enough to take care of myself.

ILDA
That's what you think.

CHARLEY
I'll be all right, Ma. Don't worry.

ILDA
I want you to write every week.

JOSE
How will you get there, Charley? By bus? (**THEY** *embrace.* **CHARLEY** *carries his steamer truck into the kitchen.* **ILDA** *packs it.* **JOSE**, **ILDA** *and* **CHARLEY** *stand together and walk out onto the sidewalk.*)

CHARLES
(*Lights up full on* **CHARLES**, *who has been watching from classroom stage right.*) Soon I would be leaving New Bedford. I would be getting on a train as a Portagee and I would be getting off that train in Ann Arbor as an American. How many Portagees could there be in the whole state of Michigan? Six or seven? Those people out there wouldn't know a Portagee if they saw one. It would be a new beginning for me. I would not be cast as a Portagee in a play whose outcome I already knew. I would be an equal.

147

(**Sound**, *Portuguese guitar music as* **Family** *stand at bus stop, and finally exit.*)

Sound: *Portuguese Guitar music. Escamil, California.* **Charles**'s *classroom.*

Charles
(*Listening to the radio in classroom.*) Senhor Fragoza once said to me, 'There are many guitars in the world, but the guitar with the sweetest sound is the Portuguese guitar.' I have heard many guitars, and Senhor Fragoza was right; the Portuguese guitar has the sweetest sound. Today I tune in to a Portuguese radio station in Morgan Hill for hours, for the infrequent pleasure of hearing the Portuguese guitar... (**He** *is interrupted by the entrance of the custodian,* **Senhor Oliveira**.)

Senhor Oliveira
(**Oliveira** *enters classroom to clean.* **He** *has a mop in his hand.*) Tell me, Mr. Felix, who was the greatest President? I think John F. Kennedy was the greatest, because he let all the Portagees into California. (*Laughs riotously.*)

Charles
(*Laughing to himself. Repeating in English.*) John F. Kennedy.

Senhor Oliveira
(*Speaking in Portuguese*) Should I mop now, or do you want to me return later. (**He** *waits for a reply.*)

Charles
(*Using sign language, etc.*) No, no. Please. Come back later... (**Harry** *enters behind* **Oliveira**.) Hey, Harry.

Oliveira
(*In Portuguese.*) Until tomorrow—se Deus quiser. (**He** *exits.*)

Beech
(*At door as* **Oliveira** *exits,* **Beech** *enters* **Charles**'s *classroom.*) Yeah, hey, how are you doing in here? We never see you!

CHARLES
Oh, yeah. I'm so busy! I never have time for anything else. Between here and my other teaching, I barely have time to do my laundry.

BEECH
Just checking.

CHARLES
(**CHARLES** *turns music off.*) So, what can I do for you, Harry?

BEECH
Not much. Just checking in, as I said. How are you doing with those Mexican kids? Did I not warn you?

CHARLES
Actually, they're great. Some of my best students.

BEECH
Are you kidding? Hmmm. What's your trick?

CHARLES
No trick. I understand them, that's all. (*Pause.*) How's your new ranch?

BEECH
(*Showing photographs of the property.*) Here it is. That's the house, and we'll keep the goats off in back, through this gate. We call it a 'Portagee gate.'

CHARLES
What? Why do you call it that?

BEECH
(*Uses board to illustrate Gate. Writes on board Portagee Gate.*)
Oh, you know. It's not made right. Just slapped together. (*Draws a picture of a Portagee Gate on the board.*) They make do with what they have...

CHARLES
Yes, they do. That could be the Portuguese creed.

BEECH
…instead of doing the job right. (*Laughing, but a bit hesitant.*) Yeah, you're right. (*Exiting. Then.*) Interesting music! It has a definite flair! (**BEECH** *gestures with his hands, flamenco style, and exits.*)

CHARLES
You, shit! (*Following* **HARRY.**) Hey, Harry!

150

BEECH
(*Returning.*) What?

CHARLES
(*Pause.*) Nothing. (**HARRY** *exits.* **CHARLES** *erases board.* **HE** *is alone in classroom.* **FRANCIS A. WALKER** *appears in balcony of auditorium.*)

WALKER
(*From auditorium balcony. Orating.*) Of the vast numbers of Poles, Bohemians, Hungarians, Russian Jews and South Italians now passing into our country, it may be said that they are mere food for contractors. Ignorant, unskilled, inert, accustomed to the beastliest conditions, with little of social aspiration, none of the expensive tastes for light and air and room, for decent dress and homely comforts, which our native people possess, and which our former immigrants so speedily acquired, the presence of hundreds of thousands of these laborers constitutes a menace to the rate of wages and to the American standard of living. This, to my mind, is absolutely appalling.

During the speech, **PODUBNIA,** **JOSE,** **CHARLES** *and* **OTHERS** *appear on the stage to listen.*

PODUBNIA
(*Enters during* **WALKER's** *speech.* **JOSE** *enters shop during speech, and listens.* **PODUBNIA** *interrupts* **WALKER's** *oration.* **CHARLES** *listens to* **PODUBNIA.**)

(*To* CHARLES, *then* WALKER.) When I came to this country, I was four-teen years old. One day I was on a boat and the next day I was working in a mill. I never had the experience of anything like that mill. What a racket in there, all the machinery going. And hot and steamy. They keep the windows closed even in the summertime so the thread won't dry out and break. I thought I had stepped into hell. Of course, I got used to it. I don't even hear the noise any more. (CHARLES *exits.* FRANCIS WALKER *exits.* PODUBNIA *enters the shop.* SHE *is stolid, expressionless, ox-like. Hands shoes to* JOSE.)

JOSE   *151*
(*Taking shoes.*) I fix them for you, Podubnia.

PODUBNIA
My husband has to have the shoes for Wednesday. He needs them for work.

JOSE
They'll be ready Tuesday, don't worry.

PODUBNIA
I don't come for them. My boy come.

JOSE
All right, Podubnia.

PODUBNIA
How much you going to charge me?

JOSE
That's seventy-five cents.

PODUBNIA
Used to be fifty cents.

JOSE
No, Podubnia. Was never fifty cents.

PODUBNIA
Was fifty cents. I remember.

JOSE
Was never fifty cents.

PODUBNIA
Was fifty cents.

JOSE

I tell you! Was never fifty cents! You been coming here all these years, Podubnia, and you still don't know my prices yet?

PODUBNIA
Was fifty cents.

JOSE
Was never fifty cents. Always has been seventy-five cents. For many years now has been seventy-five cents. You mix up the prices, Podubnia. Women's shoes, yes, fifty cents. But men's shoes, seventy-five cents. Was never fifty cents. You mix up the two shoes.

PODUBNIA
Was fifty cents.

JOSE
I tell you! Was never fifty cents! No cobbler in the city of New Bedford can fix them for fifty cents! The leather and the nails cost that much!

PODUBNIA
Was fifty cents!

JOSE
Was never fifty cents!

PODUBNIA
All right. Fix them. Seventy-five cents. (**SHE** *exits.* **JOSE** *sits alone in shop.*)

(*Lights up stage left. Scene has shifted to* BEECH'S *ranch.* BEECH *and* CHARLES *are looking out onto the property.*)

CHARLES

Gorgeous. Gorgeous property, Harry.

BEECH

Isn't it something? (*Pointing into the distance.*) There's the Gate.

CHARLES

Yeah. The Portagee gate. (**BEECH** *laughs.* **CHARLES** *stares at him.*) Harry.   *153*

BEECH

Yeah. (**CHARLES** *says nothing.*) What is it?

CHARLES

Thank you. (*Pause.*) My name is Carllllllsssssss, Harry. Can you say that? Carrrrlsssss. And I have to go. Right now. I'm expected at home. (**HE** *exits, running.*)

Lights up on New Bedford, Massachusetts. **CHARLES** *enters* **JOSE'S** *shop in old Weld Square.*

JOSE

(**JOSE** *is sitting.* **HE** *has aged considerably.* **HE** *stares at* **CHARLES**. *Then.*) Hello, Charley!

CHARLES

How's business, Pa! (**THEY** *embrace. Looking around, he sees there are no shoes on the floor waiting for repair.*) How are things going, Pa?

JOSE

All right, Charley. Everything's going good. (**HE** *tries to sound positive.* **CHARLES** *sits.*) You like California, Charley?

CHARLES

Yes. The weather's awfully nice, Pa. No snow. No ice. And it never gets too hot in the summertime.

JOSE
Are there lots of Portuguese there?

CHARLES
Yes, quite a few, Pa. They work on the ranches. Although I suppose that was mostly in the old days. I guess today they live in the towns like everybody else.

JOSE
I see that when a Portuguese here in New Bedford dies, they always list the relatives, and it seems many are now living in California. (*Pause.*) Do you have to go back to California today, Charley?

CHARLES
Yes, Pa. I am going. But I'll be back! (*Hesitates. Then.*) This is not a good place to be, Pa.

JOSE
(*Smiles, and shrugs his shoulders.*) Nothing stays the same. (**THEY** *look out onto the sidewalk together.* **SOUND** *of* **CARS** *racing back and forth over what was Weld Square.* **HE** *looks out at the new highway with a look of wonder.*) Look, Charley. Everything gone. Stores, houses, all. Who could imagine such a thing? (**CHARLES** *steps further out onto sidewalk.* **JOSE** *stays alone.*)

CHARLES
(*Stepping out. To audience.*) The superhighway sliced across Acushnet Avenue. Now he is on one side of the highway and most of his customers are on the other side. He is cut off from both vehicular and foot traffic north and west of him. Before there had been Weld Square. He was at the center of life. Weld Square was his window on the world. He could look out and see all the activity of the Square, the hustle, the bustle, the comings and goings, the happenings. He was an avid observer; no sparrow fell unnoticed. People stopped by to pass the time of day, to give him news, to tell him stories about this one and that one. He had

an eager ear for gossip. Now there is nothing to observe. Now there is no one stopping by to chat. Now, there is only this wall. (*We hear* **SOUND** *of activity on a busy street.*) I can hear the unquiet spirits of buildings and merchants crying out.
(**VIDEO IMAGES** *of the highway, busy with cars, and then of the North End of New Bedford appear through* **CHARLES**, *projecting onto the set.*)

(**CHARLES** *sees this before him.*) Over there, at the corner, is the wooden building with its magic turret from fairyland. It houses the North End Police Station on the first floor and the North End Public Library on the second floor. Over there, next to it, is the Rialto Theatre, where on Saturday afternoons I watched a Mascot serial with the Galloping Ghost himself, Red Grange. Over there is the Polish bar, Kroudvird's Shoe Store, the kosher meat market with the weird Jewish letters on its window, Tommy's Fish and Chips, Fred's Barber Shop, Phil's Cut-Rate Notions, McDermott's Fish Market with the terrible stink in the alley behind where McDermott puts all the rotting fish. Over there is Harry the Hatter. He's a very friendly guy. Over there is the Tireman. 'We fix flats! 50 cents.'

Over there is Braudy's Department Store, Inc. It's not a department store. It's just a clothing store that specializes in children's wear. Mr. Braudy runs it with the help of his wife and son. That's where my mother always brought me in late August to buy a pair of pants for the new school year. I hated to go in there with her because Mr. Braudy would poke me in the balls with the tape when he was measuring my inseam and I would be terribly embarrassed. On a weekday night Mr. Braudy took his wife to the movies at the Capitol Theatre on Acushnet Avenue near Deane Street. He bought two fifteen-cent tickets. In the middle of the picture, Mr. Braudy suddenly slumped over in his seat, dead from a heart attack. When he bought his ticket, he didn't know he wouldn't see the end of the movie. That's one of the little tricks eternity plays on us. When we're young, we think everything is fixed and in place and will go on forever. We don't know that everything is hanging by a thread. (**PROJECTIONS** *out.*)

155

JOSE
(*To* **CHARLES**.) I don't think I'll ever see you again. I don't think you'll

ever come back here again. (**THEY** *face each other as lights dim to night.* **CHARLES** *exits.* **JOSE** *locks up shop.*)

MAN
(*Lurking. Then at the door of the shop. To* **JOSE**.) Where's your money?

JOSE
Get out of here!
(**THEY** *grapple by the doorway. Suddenly the* **MAN** *breaks free and runs.* **JOSE** *looks for his money bag. It's missing. To himself.*) I got fooled. I thought he went away with nothing but I was wrong. He got my money after all. (*Slumps in doorway with a rag on his hand. After a long moment,* **IDALIA** *arrives.*)

IDALIA
(*At doorway.*) Pa! What happened? (**SHE** *struggles to help* **PA** *to his feet. Helping him stand.*) Why don't you come home now, Pa? You've worked long enough.

JOSE
 He got my money. I held on to it, but he fooled me, he got it. (*After a while.*) All right. (*Looking around.*) I've had enough. It's time to go. (*Looks around. Closes up shop.* **THEY** *walk home together. Lights dim on shop.*)

(**IDALIA** *enters kitchen.* **SHE** *sits at kitchen table.* **CHARLES** *approaches from street.*)

IDALIA
(*Looking out to him.*) Pa's gone, Charlie. (**CHARLES** *enters kitchen.* **THEY** *embrace.*) He started going downhill after that knife business. I noticed a big difference in him. You could see it. He seemed to lose interest in things.

CHARLES
How did he die?

IDALIA
He was sitting up in bed. He couldn't breathe. I knew it was coming. For two or three weeks there, I had that feeling. You just can tell.

CHARLES
So you were with him when he died?

IDALIA
Yes. I was holding him.

CHARLES
You were holding him?

IDALIA
Yes. He died in my arms. I don't know if I did the right thing. I knew he was slipping away. I could have taken him to the hospital. I thought, I'd keep him here at home with me. Let him die peacefully in his own house, in his own bed. I hope I did the right thing.

CHARLES
Yes, you did.

IDALIA
In the hospital they stick all those tubes in you. I don't think Pa would have cared for that.

CHARLES
I know he wouldn't have.

IDALIA
So I hope I made the right decision.

CHARLES
I know you made the right decision. There's no question in my mind whatsoever..
(**THEY** *look out at street*.) It's too bad they had to build that highway.

IDALIA
Well, I guess they wanted to make it easier for the tourists to get to the Cape.
(**THEY** *stand together at the doorway.* **CHARLIE** *prepares to exit.*)
(*Stopping him*) Charlie. Did you know he stopped talking before he died? We were visiting Auntie, and he said one thing to her—he said, 'Do you remember Setúbal, Mary?' That was the last thing he said. (*Pause.*) Here. I got this for you. (**SHE** *hands him* **JOSE'S** *coat. Lights out on kitchen. Up down stage center, on Airport terminal.* **CHARLES** *walks to terminal with coat.*)

CHARLES
(*Airport Terminal, in line next to* **SPANISH LADY**. **CHARLES** *speaks in Portuguese.*) Is this the line for the flight to California?

SPANISH LADY
(*Answering in Portuguese.*) Sim.

CHARLES
Are you from the Continent?

SPANISH LADY
I'm not Portuguese. I am from Spain.

CHARLES
Oh, well, they're almost the same! We're practically the same.

SPANISH LADY
No, we are not! Spain and Portugal are very different. You see, Portugal is a very poor country, and Spain is not. That has shaped the Portuguese character. They are very different from the Spanish. (*Exits to another line.*)

CHARLES
(*Ignores her. Covers self with coat.*) The smell of the shop is in the coat. The clean, bracing smell of new leather, the sheets stretched out in the

closet, the pungent smell of new rubber when you opened a Goodyear box and took out a pair of rubber heels, the metallic smell of his old tools, the knives, pliers, screwdrivers, worn to a smooth and shiny finish, the sweet smell of hot wax melting in the stitcher, the pleasant smell of shoe polish, the penetrating smell of dye, the mind-clearing smell of cement applied with a brush, the acrid, electrical smell of a shower of blue sparks crackling out of the faulty switch of his sander when he turned it on with a stick so as not to get a shock, the background smell of loose change in the cash box, dead flies in the window, thick dust on the back window, ripped-off soles and heels on the floor, worn-out shoes in a waiting pile. And I can smell him in the coat, the human smell of sweat. I can smell everything. It's like a magic coat in a fairy tale. The spirit of the shop, the spirit of my father is with me, covering me, protecting me. (*Lights down on Airport Terminal.*)

159

ESCAMIL, CALIFORNIA
(**CHARLES** *enters classroom in California. Hangs up coat, and turns on radio. Fado music is playing.* **HE** *sits and types, listening to the music.*)

SENHOR OLIVEIRA
(*Enters and listens to music.* **HE** *begins to mop floor. After a while, speaking Portuguese.*)
Where was your father born?

CHARLES
(*During the scene,* **OLIVEIRA** *speaks mainly in Portuguese, and* **CHARLES** *speaks mainly in English, with more Portuguese added as the end of the play nears. In English.*) My father was born in Setúbal.

SENHOR OLIVEIRA
(*In Portuguese.*) That is on the Continent.

CHARLES
(*In English.*) Yes. It's on the Continent.

OLIVEIRA
Have you ever gone back there to visit his birthplace?

CHARLES
No, I never have.

OLIVEIRA
This summer, during the vacation, why don't you go? I think it would be nice for you to visit the land of your father.

CHARLES
I can't go. (*Speaking hesitantly in non-native Portuguese*) *Não posso.*

OLIVEIRA
Why not?

CHARLES
I don't have the money. *Não tenho dinheiro.*

OLIVEIRA
(*Riotous laughter.*) *Oh homem, tu não me digas isso. 'Tás cheio de dinheiro!*

CHARLES
I have plenty of money?

OLIVEIRA
Yes! *Eu conheço a tua manha! Tu não me enganas! Eu não sou um nenhum bebé. Podes enganar outros, mas a mim não!* You no fool me.

CHARLES
The truth of the matter is I am in debt. (**LIGHTS** *dim to end of play.*) *Como é que sabe que tenho dinheiro?*

OLIVEIRA
Eu sei! I know! *Olha só pró teu carro; tem 20 anos de idade. É um piece-a-junk a cair aos bocados. Eu sei porque é. É porque estás a guardar o dinheiro todo na algibeira.* (**HE** *holds a fistful of imaginary greenbacks by his face and then shoves the fist deep down into an imaginary pocket that extends to his knee.*) *Não, não, não sou nenhum bebé! Se não, para onde é*

que vai o dinheiro?

CHARLES
Vai p'ra a comida. Vai p'ra a gasolina. Vai p'ra as lições de música da minha filha. Um milhão de coisas. Vai todo porque a minha família não vive como os portugueses. We live like Americans!

Lights to black.

END OF PLAY